What the Pros Say about Lore

My admiration for Byron Nelson, both as a golfer and as a wonderful gentleman has virtually spanned my lifetime. As a boy I read what Byron wrote about his ideas on the golf swing and how he had come up in the game from his own boyhood days in the caddie years of Texas to such great success on the pro tour. I was particularly impressed with the way he treated the game with such grace, dignity, and respect. This all had a great impact on me, little ever thinking that in the years to come I would become a good friend of this kindly man and enjoy time with him when we were together at golf events. All the players of my generation looked up to Byron Nelson and all that he stood for and contributed to our great game.

Arnold Palmer
Professional Golfer and Friend

I loved Byron Nelson as a friend, teacher, and confidant. The most unusual quality I saw in Byron was his sense of humor and fun. He really liked to ham it up on the golf course. What I learned from him was how to speak in front of people. His honesty and humility were the canvas from which he spoke. Byron to me epitomized what is right with the human race.

Tom Watson
Professional Golfer and Friend

Byron was a role model in every sense of the word to me as a golfer, husband, and most importantly, as a man. He had the most genuine compassion I have ever seen in a man. From him I learned a lot about the meaning of the word *humble*. Byron could have been the greatest golfer ever, but you would have no idea of that from his behavior. He is the one man after whom every man could model his life. He was spiritual, humble, a great golfer, a fabulous husband and philanthropist, and mostly, a great mentor to many.

Corey Pavin
Professional Golfer and Friend

Once I became a club professional, Byron was a huge help to me. When I'd ask him to come out for some special event, he came every single time. He's the only pro I know who would go out of his way to help raise money or do something else to help golf, and of course, his presence always made each event a success.

Ross T. Collins
Professional Golfer and National Left-Handed Golf Champion

We were doing the Junior Clinic at Byron's tournament one year when Tom Watson challenged Byron to hit his driver off the grass and hit the 200-yard sign. Byron said okay, and he hit it right in the middle. As people clapped wildly, Byron walked over to me and said humbly, "Do you believe I did that?" He had it all—class, talent, entertainment, and yet so humble!

D. A. Weibring
Professional Golfer, Friend, and Partner in Golf Design

Life with Lord Byron

To. Joe Doramus

Happy Golfing
&
Happy Days!

Peggy Nelson

Life with Lord Byron

Laughter, Romance &
Lessons Learned from
Golf's Greatest Gentleman

PEGGY NELSON

CREATIVE ENTERPRISES STUDIO

Fort Worth, TX 76022

Life with Lord Byron
Peggy Nelson

Published with Creative Enterprises Studio, 1507 Shirley Way, Fort Worth, TX 76022. CreativeEnterprisesLtd.com

All author royalties and profits from this book are dedicated to the Byron Nelson Marital Trust.

All stories from professional athletes, friends, and family are used with written permission.

Byron Nelson Remembers 1945 © 1995, 2010 The Byron Nelson Foundation. Used by permission. All rights reserved.

All photographs used with permission of the copyright holders.

Interior Design: Inside Out Design & Typsetting, Hurst, Texas

Cover Design: The Dugan Design Group

Cataloging in Publication Data
Nelson, Peggy.
    Life with Lord Byron : laughter, romance, and lessons learned from golf's greatest gentleman / Peggy Nelson.
        p.   cm.
    Includes bibliographical references.
    ISBN 978-0-9826143-0-3 (tradepaper)
1. Nelson, Byron, 1912–2006. 2. Golfers—United States—Biography. I. Title.
GV946.N45 2010
796.352092–dc22
[B]   2010003261

Printed in the United States of America
10 11 12 13 14 15 TS 6 5 4 3 2 1

To Byron,
my hero, my sweetheart, my inspiration
for twenty beautiful years,
and to his many friends and fans
around the world

Contents

Foreword   xi

Acknowledgments   xiii

Prologue: A Cinderella Story   xv

1   Byron Nelson—Who's He?   1

2   The Letter   9

3   The First Eighteen Is the Hardest   15

4   Sixteen Things   21

5   Texas Tee Off   29

6   One Wonderful Wedding Day   39

7   Moving to Fairway Ranch   47

8   The Great Piano Saga   57

9   How to Play Golf with Your Spouse   67

Contents

10   An Unforgettable Secretary's Day   77

11   The Only One Who Never Disappointed Me   83

12   The Pro and the Pros   93

13   Isn't He a Rascal?   101

14   No Wonder They Call You "Lord"   113

15   When Admitting a Mistake Changed Lives   123

16   The Master Craftsman   131

17   Wait, This Guy's in Terrible Trouble!   145

18   Winning the Final Round   155

19   Aftermath and Media   165

Epilogue: Back in the Clubhouse   177

About the Author   187

Byron Nelson Remembers 1945   189

Foreword

When Peggy asked me to write a foreword to this book, my head started to spin, trying to think of which superlatives I would use to describe Byron. Most of them have been used before, and I agree with all the kind words spoken and written about Byron. I never heard a negative word about him or ever heard him say a negative word about anybody else. Byron was the nicest, kindest, most caring, and most giving human being I have ever met. He was truly a man of God! I wanted to be around him with the hope he would rub off on me. I think most people he encountered felt exactly the same way.

We first met in 1980 at the Byron Nelson Golf Classic and Preston Trail Golf Club. At the time I looked up to him because of his unbelievable golf accomplishments. Byron was nice enough to offer his help to me. He called me and wanted to meet me on the driving range at Preston Trail. You can just imagine my excitement! We were there for about five minutes when the head pro informed Byron that I needed to be twenty-one years old to be on the property. I was shocked that the club wouldn't allow Lord Byron to have me there. Byron was kind enough to take me over to Northwood Country Club, and we played eighteen holes.

What a great day it turned out to be! Byron was sixty-eight years old, but you could still see his greatness as a golfer thirty-four years after he had retired. That day I learned that "golf legend" was just a small part of who Byron Nelson really was. Byron gave of himself and cared deeply for those around him. He wrote me about thirty different notes. Some were for a job "well done," some for "you're going in the right direction," and some said "keep your head up." Every note was very special to me. I think Byron wrote notes to many PGA Tour players. He was really a true gentleman.

In 2007, the year after Byron's death, I was fortunate enough to win the EDS Byron Nelson Championship. It was a lifelong dream come true. Ironically it was the first Nelson Championship without Byron in attendance. Even though physically Byron wasn't there, he was there with me spiritually and emotionally. I have no doubt I got a little help from above.

It is my honor to be associated with Byron, to even have been considered a friend. Byron Nelson was the ultimate role model— great golf champion, even greater champion at life!

Scott Verplank
Professional Golfer

Acknowledgments

Writing a book is a daunting project in many ways, and this one could never have happened without the encouragement of many friends and family. While I knew our story was a delightful one from Byron's and my viewpoint, it only recently occurred to me that it might have a wider application for many of Byron's fans, who would like to know more about him.

Next, there are the many folks from all walks of life who added their own unique perspectives, great stories, and insights that have helped me appreciate that wonderful man even more than I already did.

Also, I'm amazingly grateful to Mary Hollingsworth, who took a gander at my initial manuscript and said, "You've got a book here, girl!" Mary, you're a wonder, and it's been an entertaining and productive trip with you and the Creative Enterprises Studio team.

Most of all, I'm indebted forever and always to my Lord, who took hold of my life all those years ago and gave me Byron to love and to cherish.

I truly am the most blessed woman in all the world.

Prologue

A Cinderella Story

Did you grow up reading fairy tales? Probably not, if you're a guy. But lots of girls like me did. The difference was that I kind of, sort of, halfway, *almost* believed them to be true. For sure I wanted to believe the happily-ever-after part.

Real life being what it is, I had many occasions to learn that a fairy-tale love might not be true for me. One crush after another did not bloom into a forever romance. Then marital mistakes on my part should have shown me I needed to have God involved to get to the happy, fairy-tale ending. It seemed I was being forced to the unpleasant conclusion that perhaps *Cinderella* was really just fiction after all.

Yet some deep-down part of me did not want to give up on romance, even though by the time I was thirty-seven, evidence was only confirming that my dream was just that—a dream. But life (and the Lord) has a way of surprising us. And because many (okay, eight or ten) folks have encouraged, nudged, and downright insisted I write it all down, I'm finally doing it. But not just for me. I am writing because it may be a blessing to you to know that as much as you admired and respected Byron, as much as the world thought they knew him, he was actually even better than that. And you deserve to know that he was even more amazing to live with than to admire from afar.

Another, and perhaps more important, reason for writing our story is that someone, somewhere, reading it may want to learn from and try to do the things that Byron did and said, if not in golf, then perhaps in life in general or in their own marriages, or in preparing for that big step. As Byron would say to people who were newly married, "If you're half as happy as we are, you'll be happy enough!"

This book may also be useful for young folks who are a long way from being married or even wanting to become so, because if you choose to learn from Byron now when you are young, you will find it much easier to grow into the kind of man or woman the good Lord intends for you to become. I'm living proof of that.

Lucky me, I did get to live my dream for twenty years with this gentle champion and prince. Now I invite you into the home of my heart to let you know a little more about Byron, what he was like to live with and love every single day of our very blessed time together.

Peggy Nelson

I never thought I was any different from or better than anyone else just because I played a little golf over fifty years ago. But people treat me that way, and all I can do is to be grateful and try hard to deserve it.

—Byron Nelson, 2000

1

Byron Nelson—Who's He?

The day before I met Byron, I had never even heard of him. I suppose that could be said by lots of folks twenty-four hours before they met someone very special. But in this case he was a world-famous golfer, and though I was barely a beginner, I should have had at least some inkling of who he was.

When I say I was just a beginner at golf, I should be completely truthful and say I pretty much hated the game. The main reason I was even giving it a shot was that I worked for NCR Corporation as retail advertising manager, and they had a couple of nearly free employee golf courses at NCR Country Club (no tennis, no swimming, just golf, thank you). I actually did play tennis and softball at the time and loved both sports, so golf had no appeal for me at first. In fact, I had a rough start. The first few times I tried to play a full eighteen, I walked—no, stomped—off the course in the middle of the round out of sheer frustration. The huge, beautiful old trees, acres of lush green grass, and gently rolling hills—all the ambience for which golf courses are famous—did not make as much of an impression on me as the triple, quadruple, and quintuple bogeys that comprised most of my beginning scores.

Somewhere in those early rounds, though, I made my first birdie on a tough par five (don't tell anyone I didn't realize at first what a miracle I had performed!), and the hook began to sink in. Still, when I heard that someone named Byron Nelson would be giving a clinic, whatever that was, at something called the "Bogey Busters" at my club, my first thought was, *Who's he?* After all I had barely heard of the more contemporary pros at that time, such as Jack Nicklaus, Tom Watson, and Lee Trevino, and I certainly was not spending my weekends watching golf on television, unless I needed a nap.

After learning a little about Byron's many golf records and accomplishments on and off the course, though, I decided to take the day off from work and go see this great legend. Bear in mind that I was not expecting to learn anything, because I hardly knew how to find my way around the course, and I didn't even know enough to ask halfway intelligent questions of someone as famous as this Nelson guy.

I Want to See Your Eyes

So there I was with about a hundred other folks, gathered around the spot where they were setting up for this clinic thing. It took place on the tenth tee of the South Course, the one where I later learned

Raymond Floyd had won the PGA Championship in 1969. The South is truly a championship venue with rolling hills and several awesome bunkers. There are no water hazards, but lots of enormous oak and maple trees tower over narrow fairways and surround well-placed greens guarded by several fearsome sand bunkers. The clinic was cohosted by Eddie Merrins, UCLA's golf coach and the pro at Bel Air Country Club in Beverly Hills.

I heard a little commotion and turned to see an older man strolling out of the clubhouse toward us. Wearing a handsome straw fedora, he looked very kind, with an expression on his face that could best be described as a gentle, patient smile. Then I realized it must be the Byron Nelson I had come to see. The Hat, I learned later, was the one folks saw him wearing most everywhere he went. It was part of his famous persona.

Soon Mr. Nelson and Mr. Merrins began the clinic, demonstrating swing flaws, chip shots, draws, fades, slices, and hooks. Of course I didn't have a clue what they were even talking about. When the clinic was over and the golfers got ready to play, I decided to follow Mr. Nelson along the course, because it would probably be the only time I would ever get to see a true golf legend play up close and personal.

The format for this two-day event was nine holes one day on one course and nine holes the next day on the other, with various celebrities in addition to Byron playing with groups of three amateurs. Among the celebrities were Johnny Bench, Spanky McFarland, then Vice President George H. W. Bush, and others. The whole affair was more of a private party hosted by local industrialist Cy Laughter, so there were no tickets sold or gallery ropes to separate the small clusters of spectators from the players, though the public was welcome to attend. And since it took place on a Monday and Tuesday, rather than a weekend, it didn't draw a huge audience. In fact Byron had finished his television golf commentating more than seven years earlier, so other than the tournament with his name on it in Dallas, he was somewhat relegated to old news status, except for the more knowledgeable golf fans, and I could hardly be said to fit in that category.

Byron's group began play that gorgeous, blue-sky day on the tenth tee of the North Course. As he waited for his team to tee off, Byron leaned easily on his driver and glanced casually around the ten or fifteen folks watching. When he came to me, his gaze paused just long enough for me to think, *That man has the bluest eyes I've ever seen!* Then he stepped up, confidently hit his drive, and off they went. I didn't know enough about the game then to even have a clue what a good swing or great shot looked like, but since I had taken the whole day off, I was determined to walk the nine and watch what this world champion did.

As they finished the tenth hole and moved to the short par three eleventh, I chose a spot on the twelfth—a dogleg par five—where I would have a better view of the play. I was standing in the rough, hopefully out of the range of any errant amateur tee shots, and got to see Mr. Nelson hit his drive straight down the middle of the fairway. But instead of walking to his ball—the standard procedure—he seemed to be heading directly toward me. I was startled when he walked right up to me and said, "Would you please take off your sunglasses? I want to see your eyes."

Thunderstruck! Stunned. Amazed, I took off my sunglasses and looked at him while he studied me.

Then he said, "Thank you very much," went back to his ball, and kept playing.

It was odd, for sure, and without a doubt the most astonishing thing that had ever happened to little old ordinary me. Years later, after we were married, he said that he was almost as startled as I was when he did that, because he had never done anything like it before or since. And as we have told our story through the years, anyone who knew him well would ask, "Byron did that?" in a tone of shocked surprise.

But let's get back to golf. Sometime after Byron hit his next couple of shots, he asked if I played, and I shyly replied, "Not exactly," confessing that I was just a beginner and did not like it much. We visited a little more off and on while he played with his group, and when we were walking up toward the clubhouse, he asked if I was coming back the next day.

"I can't," I replied. "I have to work."

Then he looked straight at me and said, "Please come back."

Now to those who might be thinking, *whoopee* or *hey-hey*, you need to know there was nothing more to his request than that he had enjoyed talking to me. I certainly did not see why he would, but I admit I was so pleased by this champion's invitation that I quickly decided at least to take my lunch hour the next day and enjoy a little more golf.

> Byron was a legend and a giant in our sport, yet he was big enough to be small and strong enough to show genuine, sincere kindness to all—an unbelievable human being! Byron's records may never be broken. But that's not why I admired him. It was *who* he was, not *what* he was. Anyone who was blessed to know Byron knows what I mean. He was, along with my father, my hero.
>
> *Greg Hopkins*
> *President and CEO*
> *Cleveland Golf*

I Have a New Golf Hero

The next day was just as memorable, because when I showed up on the first tee of the South Course (the site for not only the PGA Championship in 1969, but also for the U.S. Women's Open in 1986 won by Jane Geddes), Mr. Nelson was surprised to see me. I explained that I was on my lunch hour, but I must admit that it became a rather long lunch, because I followed my new golf hero the full nine holes, and I was delightedly surprised when, on one long par five, after he hit his drive straight and true down the middle of a very tight fairway, he looked over at me, smiled, and said, "I hit that one just for you." Imagine!

As we all toiled up the hill toward the clubhouse at the end of the nine holes, Byron's admiring fans began to crowd around him for autographs, but I just shook his hand, said thank you, and melted into the crowd. Oddly I remember, with no reason for it at all, when he let go of my hand, I felt I was being torn in two. Very mysterious.

A few days afterward, I wrote the second fan letter of my life to Mr. Nelson (I had to call information to get his address) and sent it off, not expecting to hear anything back. But shortly I received his handwritten note, saying he had enjoyed meeting me and hoped I would like learning to play golf. Several weeks later, after boring friends and colleagues to tears with the whole story, I decided to send Mr. Nelson a book of hilarious short stories about golf by my favorite author at the time, P. G. Wodehouse—the writer to whom I had sent my first fan letter many years earlier. I didn't know then that Byron actually had very little interest in reading about golf. In any case, figuring that he might not remember who I was, since he no doubt met hundreds of people a year, I put my business card in the book. That was June 1981, and that was it. I learned much later that he had tried to call my office to thank me for the book (which he never did read), but I was out of town on a business trip.

As mentioned earlier, the golf hook had begun to get into my psyche just a little, and Mr. Nelson's encouragement no doubt motivated me to keep at it. I soon found a nine-hole ladies' evening group, and first softball and then tennis fell off the edge of my personal sports universe. Over the next couple of years, I became more and more consumed with playing golf, though I advanced only as far as group lessons and not very much practice, so on the few days when I was able to play eighteen holes, I had not even come within a driver's length of breaking a hundred.

My favorite memory of Byron was a round of golf I played with Byron and Peggy in Florida. There were just the three of us, and on the first tee Byron said with a twinkle in his eyes, "Peggy and I always play together as a team . . . and we get our full handicap." They beat me easily, but it was a memorable round of golf. I was playing to a four back then, but Byron never said a thing about my game until I asked him why my misses always seemed to go to the right. He said, "You're not setting your club properly at the top." My next drive was perfect, and Byron just nodded his head in approval. I'll never forget that one-sentence lesson.

Frank Houseman
Salesmanship Club Tournament Chairman 1996 and 1997
President 1999

2

The Letter

Four years went by, and in October 1985, I was watching a golf tournament on television when one of the commentators said, "We want to express our condolences to Byron Nelson on the death of his wife, Louise, after a long illness." I'd had no idea, of course, and thought about sending him a sympathy card, but I figured he wouldn't remember who I was. Besides I didn't have his address anymore, so I thought no more about it.

Then came March 1986, nearly five years after that first meeting. I was a freelance writer, having gone through nearly every advertising agency in Dayton like an avenging flame. I was also on quite a strenuous spiritual journey. Having grown up in the Catholic church, but being disconnected from all religion for more than fifteen years, I had been attending a nearby Methodist church just long enough to decide that God was calling me to be a Methodist minister. Pretty scary. I had taken courses at a local seminary, including the gospel of Mark, the Psalms, Methodist history, even a year of Greek, and preaching. That last one was what did me in, because at a visceral level I simply knew this was *not* what God had in mind for me. So I was truly at a crossroads. I clearly remember looking up at the ceiling in my living room and saying out loud, "Okay, God, what do you want me to do?"

No answer. But the next day, March 14, a letter dropped through my mail slot that stunned me. It was from Mr. Nelson himself, saying he was coming back to Dayton in June for that same golf event and would like for me to come out and see him play. Amazing! I was astonished he even remembered me. I was also thrilled, especially since I at least now had hopes of some day breaking a hundred and could tell him I had birdied a par five (leaving out that I once also made a ten on a par three by picking up my ball after nine feckless shots and throwing it in the cup).

So I sat down to write a reply. Wanting to make a good impression, I used my very best penmanship (none too good, even when I'm not nervous) and wrote a charming response. I read it. Then it went into the wastebasket as being beyond ridiculous. So I started over. Another wastebasket entry. Three. Four. (Did I mention I once was an English major?) Finally I managed to write one that wasn't too juvenile, goofy, silly, or all of the above. It went into the mail. A few days later, as I returned home from a freelance writing assignment, I checked my answering machine and heard that strong, deep voice from five years before. I could not believe Byron Nelson would actually call me! I danced around the room, excited as a kid at Christmas. Wow.

That was the start of a unique fan-celebrity friendship, or so we both thought for a while. More letters and phone calls came and went over the next two months, and it was amazing how long we talked on the phone. Of course women are notably more verbal, and I've never had trouble conversing, but Byron was so easy to talk to and seemed to enjoy hearing about my golf hits and misses. I learned later that he had never talked on the phone like that with anyone, and he had the highest phone bills of his life over the next six months!

I'm Coming to Play Golf with You

Life rolled along, with freelance work keeping me somewhat gainfully employed, and my golf at least getting a wee bit better. Then around May 20, Byron called to say this: "I'm going to be in New York for a few days before I come to Dayton for the Bogey Busters. I have an extra day that I could stay there, but I would rather come to Dayton earlier and play golf with you."

I nearly dropped the phone! Visualizing a nightmare round on my part and my hero shooting sixty-three or so, I stammered, "Oh, you don't want to do that—I'm really not very good."

Byron replied with a smile in his voice, "Oh, I'm just a plain old Joe. We'll just go have a good time."

I had to acquiesce, though I was pretty sure which of us would be having the least good time at that point. Actually I had been working pretty hard on my game by then, playing a couple of times a week and practicing a lot. Now with the added incentive of playing with Mr. Nelson himself, I ramped it up quite a bit. I went out to hit balls at 6:30 in the morning, played even more, and oddly enough thought I was getting quite a bit better. That was until the day I rashly took on the championship South Course and added up some incomprehensible numbers, including a couple of tens and a thirteen on the eighteenth. Dragging my oxygen-starved body off the last green, I dropped down on a bench and put my head in my hands, saying to myself, *What was I thinking, trying to play golf with him?*

The next weekend was Jack Nicklaus's Memorial Tournament in Columbus, so I decided to go. After I got to the course, it suddenly occurred to me, *I wonder if he's here?* Byron had not said anything about it nor had I mentioned that I would be there, but as I walked over toward the eighteenth green where everything was set up for the opening ceremony, I saw . . . The Hat.

Suddenly I was more excited than I had been in all my life, while at the same time wondering why. After all, I had never been a fan-celebrity-type person, plus he was more than thirty years older than I was, so it wasn't as if I was thinking romance, for goodness' sake. But I began working my way around the crowd on the hill in front of the clubhouse until I got as close as I could and sat down on the soft green grass. I focused on Byron as the speakers did their parts, and as I watched him and wondered what in the world was going on, it hit me right between the eyes . . .

I'm in Love with This Old Guy!

Thunderstruck again! So that's what all the excitement was about. It was not a fan-celebrity thing, as I had thought, but something definitely, completely different.

Once the speeches were over and the fans again began to line up for Byron's autograph, it was almost a déjà vu for me of the last time I had seen him five years before when I said a quick good-bye as I left the golf course. Only this time I was saying hello again with my heart in an entirely new place—not that I had any idea whether his emotions were the same. In fact, as I moved up in the line, I had a moment of panic, thinking he might be remembering me as a tall, blue-eyed blonde or some such vision. And earlier that particular day it had been misting heavily before the sun finally broke through, so my long, shaggy, curly perm gave me the remarkable look of a wet poodle.

Nevertheless, I finally stepped forward to shake his hand, saying, "I don't need your autograph, Mr. Nelson—I'm Peggy."

Apparently blue-eyed blonde was not what he remembered at all, and as he signed the last autograph and handed it back to the young fan, he started firing questions at me: "Did I tell you my flight number? Are you going to pick me up at the airport next week?" The next thing I knew, his arm was around my waist, and he was propelling me through the crowd to where the Champions' Clinic was to be held at the practice range.

About that time a young man in suit and tie approached and said, "Mr. Nelson, Mr. Nicklaus is having the Captains' Club meeting now."

Byron firmly replied, "I'm not going."

I remember the expression on that fellow's face to this day as he realized he had to go back to Jack Nicklaus and tell him the 1980 Honoree was not going to appear. It reminded me of the expression on the face of Darth Vader's hapless lieutenant in *Star Wars* when he had to give his boss some bad news.

We continued walking toward the practice range, and who was coming down the steps but Hale Irwin. He saw Byron, then me, and Hale's eyebrows began an upward climb of surprise. Then Byron hailed him and introduced us, and I guess it was clear to Hale that something was going on. I learned later that many of the pros had been worried about Byron ever since Louise had died, because he had seemed to lose his bearings in his grief, had dropped thirty pounds, and even his family doctor had told him, "Byron, we're going to have to do something or you're not going to make it."

At the time all I could see was that Hale seemed pleased, if surprised, to meet this wet-poodle person, and off Byron and I went to see the clinic. Peter Jacobsen entertained everyone with his impressions of Craig Stadler and Arnold Palmer, among others, and when it was over, Byron gave me a sweet peck on the cheek and said, "See you next week."

Indeed. It seemed the fan-celebrity thing was not working for him anymore either. He was seventy-four. I was forty-one. Astonishing!

Peggy and I love to shop, and Byron always enjoyed seeing the results of our expeditions. That included putting on a fashion show that never failed to produce a sparkle in his eyes as he watched Peggy. His love for her was as big as Texas and more—it just spilled out constantly!

Judy Stead
Peggy's Best Friend since 1962

3

The First Eighteen Is the Hardest

Now to that round of golf with Byron. As you might imagine, I was not looking forward to it. In fact, I prayed harder than ever in my life that it would rain absolute buckets that day, and as I drove to the airport to meet Mr. Nelson, I was delighting in the forecast that promised an 80 percent chance of rain. I was buoyed further by the ominously black sky as I parked my car. No way would we be playing golf today, no possibility of embarrassing myself in front of this larger-than-life golfer.

God is good, I said to myself as I walked into the terminal.

Meeting Byron at his gate and taking the escalator with him down to baggage claim, I looked up into those blue eyes, tried to sound disappointed, and said, "Mr. Nelson, I should tell you there's an 80 percent chance of rain today."

He just smiled and replied, "That means there's a 20 percent chance it won't."

And it didn't. That should have told me right then, Byron had an uncanny way of being right nearly all the time about almost everything.

A Small Reprieve

I drove him to his hotel, waited while he checked in, and off we went to the golf course. But first I got a small reprieve, because Byron said he was hungry and asked if we could stop for breakfast.

"Sure," I said, grateful for the delay since it was now sunny skies everywhere I looked, and my doom was obviously sealed.

We went into the restaurant and were seated, and then things started to get weird. The waitress approached, asked if we wanted coffee, we both said yes, she set the cups and saucers down, then asked Byron if he wanted cream or sugar.

He replied, "No, I take my coffee black, thank you."

Now it was my turn, and I had always liked my coffee with cream. No sugar, just cream. What did I say to the waitress? "Black is fine, thank you." I remember wondering what had made me say that.

Then we were both sipping our hot, black coffee and I, still feeling awkward in the presence of this great man of golf, attempted some golf-type conversation. I picked the topic of golf gloves.

"Byron, I notice the pros on television always wear a golf glove, and I was wondering, do you wear one?" Mind you, I had been wearing one myself for a while, even though I didn't much like it because the gloves were expensive, got dirty really fast, didn't last long, and got hot in all but the coldest months of the golf season.

And back then you couldn't wash and reuse them as you can the high-tech ones of today.

Byron replied, "No, never wore one. They're too expensive, get all dirty, don't last long, and I had a pretty good grip, so I didn't need one." Then he looked at me and said, "Do you wear one?"

And I instantly replied, "No, not me."

There you have it: inside of two minutes' time, I had lied to Lord Byron, as he was called on the circuit. Twice! What in the world had happened to the independent-minded, semi-feminist person known as me? My mind was in a whirl.

Teeing Off with Byron

Other than my new penchant for prevaricating, the breakfast was delightful, and soon we were on our way to the first tee at NCR Country Club, where the pro, Jeff Steinberg, was waiting for us. I had at least had the good sense to alert him that Byron was coming and to let him know not to noise it about, because I certainly did not want a crowd around for my first drive in front of Byron Nelson and possibly the entire membership, their spouses, and a gaggle of children.

As luck (and the Lord) would have it, I hit a whopper of a drive, for me at least. It sailed high off the elevated tee and far down the hill, tailing off just a touch to the right and a few feet into the rough. Byron looked surprised, though my subsequent play lived up to my earlier bad expectations. I remember very little of that round, other than just enjoying being with him and wishing I could play better. But he didn't seem to care about my score at all, though he did show me a great chipping technique I could do with my six-iron when I was close to the green but a ways from the pin. It's come in handy many times since.

About the rest of his stay, I don't recall a lot. The Bogey Busters event that year was played at a different course, and naturally I went out to follow my hero. As it happened, Byron was paired with none other than Johnny Mathis, the singing legend and a great part of my high school fantasy life from twenty years before. Here I was with two celebrities, pretty tongue-tied, and living in a state of suspended animation, wondering, *Will I ever recover from this out-of-body experience?*

The Start of Something Wonderful

Byron was by nature an optimist who knew just the right thing to say to encourage his friends, family, and especially me. It showed in every area of his life, and he was not only romantic, but enthusiastically so. In fact, the very first time he kissed me, he took me in his arms and kissed me thoroughly and well. Then he stepped back, still holding on to my shoulders, smiled, and said, "I *knew* it would be like that!"

Wow! I thought, *I've never gotten a rave review before.* And I'd recommend the same approach to young folks falling in love, because this response will motivate him—or her—to get even better.

By the time Byron flew back to Texas, we both knew we had the start of a wonderful friendship . . . that was rapidly becoming far more serious. The phone calls and letters came and went more often now, and soon we were talking about marriage, even though this was just July and August, only a couple of months after we had reconnected five years after our first meeting.

Every so often in your life you get to meet someone who leaves a huge impact on you. Byron Nelson was one of those people to me. I was fortunate enough to meet Byron during his tournament in 1987, and from the moment I met him, I realized he was a very special person. His humility and incredible love for life and people were the first impressions he left with me. However it was only in the early '90s that I really got to know Byron well.

After one round during his tournament in Dallas, he came up to me and asked if we could spend ten minutes together. I had not putted particularly well that day but had struck the ball beautifully. I didn't realize Byron had been watching me from the CBS tower on the eighteenth. I was only too pleased to have the opportunity to spend some time with him. A few minutes later he came down to the locker room, and we went to the indoor pool area and sat down on a bench. For the next hour and a half, Byron and I talked about putting and about the game in general. He was so positive about my game and my putting and just told me to be patient, as it would all fall into place if I wanted it badly enough! We spoke about a great many things during that time, but when someone of Byron's stature compliments you on your game . . . well, it meant the world to me.

From that day on, every time I played well in an event, Byron would write me a note complimenting me on how well I had played, but more importantly, how much he admired my attitude and conduct on the course. I have kept all of the notes he wrote me and they are some of my prized possessions!

Nick Price
Professional Golfer, Byron Nelson Tournament Champion 1991
PGA Championship and British Open Winner

4

Sixteen Things

One day Byron called with a more serious tone in his voice than usual. He said he had something he wanted to tell me, and I smilingly responded, "Is this serious?"

He replied that since we were talking about marriage, he realized I had led a fairly sheltered life, and if I were to marry him, a lot of things would change. So he had started making a list of all those considerations, and when he was ready, he would call and tell me.

"Okay," I replied, wondering but not worried. Honestly I've never been very good at worrying about things. I tend to lose focus on whatever it was I began to worry about and then give up.

A few days later Byron reported that he had his list ready and wanted to come tell me about it and see what I thought.

"How many things are on this list?" I asked.

"Sixteen," he replied, and I did have to take a deep breath at that.

But the next week he came to town, I met him at the airport, and we went to Aullwood Gardens, one of my favorite spots in Dayton. We sat on two lawn chairs, and he pulled a yellow legal pad out of his briefcase and began.

I didn't keep that piece of paper, unfortunately, so I don't recall the whole list of concerns, but among them were his family, Louise's family, and my having to leave not only Ohio but also my friends and my children (though the boys were already either away at college or about to go). Then there was the church he attended, which was a little nervous about divorced folks. Next came his celebrity status— that basically every time he set foot off the ranch, he was in the public eye, and he took that responsibility very seriously indeed. He was also aware that his mother had exhibited signs of mental failing from the time she was eighty-five, so he figured he could count on, Lord willing, ten years of good mental faculties, but of course it was a concern of his. Then there was the Byron Nelson tournament, travel, and the fact that while he was comfortable financially, we would not have a lot of money to throw around and would need to be careful to some degree.

Another item was his concern that it was not fair to me to be married to someone so much older, with all the potential problems that could eventually entail. He said he had prayed hard about this one, but he knew that he loved me and felt I loved him enough to take good care of him when the need arose.

Finally, after he had gone over every item and answered the few questions I had, he asked me, "After all this, do you still want to marry me?

"More than ever," I firmly replied.

Strangely, it did not occur to me until years later that *Byron* was taking a huge risk in marrying *me*. Not only was his church leery of folks like me who had been divorced, but there were certainly some who would be thinking he had gone off his rocker marrying someone so much younger, who might potentially be after his money if he had any, or the ranch, or just wanting to escape Ohio winters. Actually, at that point Byron had no endorsements or other income from his golf career, so that was not an issue.

In truth, he was risking even more than that—his lifelong reputation as a wise, thoughtful, solid Christian man. He also could lose not only his church family but also his own and Louise's families, as well as many dear friends. In fact, one close confidant did advise him to have a prenuptial agreement in place before the wedding.

Byron's response: "I know her. I don't need that."

And I would have to agree that, based on a combination of my total naiveté and my complete trust in him, Byron was right.

Byron and My Family

While we had a whirlwind courtship, Byron certainly covered all the bases in his wonderful way. He had met both of my boys, even attending Stan's high school graduation, much to Stan's horror.

"Mom, you're not going to make him sit through four hours of sheer torture, are you?" But he came and actually seemed to enjoy it.

One memorable day Byron called and said, "I want you to know one thing: I love you, and your boys are part of you, so I love them too." No conditions, no qualifications, just pure acceptance and love from the beginning. I found out that not only did he mean it, but also he truly enjoyed the boys and the vitality they brought to his life, as well as some pretty hilarious moments.

One Saturday morning, for instance, I was out on the weekly doughnut run when Byron called. John answered the phone half asleep, as he had been out late with his friends the night before. Byron proceeded to tell John that when I came to Texas and married him, he was going to take very good care of me and do his best to make me happy.

John replied, "You'd better," and hung up. Then he woke up completely, horrified at what he had just done. Fortunately, Byron sat there in Texas just chuckling to himself.

The Chief Cook and the Dishwasher

Another time that clever fellow inquired on the phone, "Do you like to cook?" I replied enthusiastically in the affirmative and promised to send him my culinary résumé, in which I rashly claimed to make the best popcorn in five counties. That intrigued him because he had never eaten popcorn much. Later I realized how wise his phrasing was, because while many women are great cooks, they don't necessarily want to make three meals a day forever. And he knew for sure that because Louise had been a wonderful cook, he wanted to count on three good meals a day.

I find cooking therapeutic—"playing with food," I call it. And

Byron enjoyed the results. A little later on, before I moved to Texas, Byron promised me that if I cooked, he would do the dishes. And he said that he didn't have a dishwasher, but he would get one if I wanted it. I didn't want a dishwasher, though, because before I had gotten one in my Ohio kitchen, my boys and I had shared those duties, and while we were washing and drying, we would talk about what was going on at school, with their friends, sports, all kinds of things. When the "magical" dishwasher came in, obviously, just one person was needed, so those sweet conversations stopped.

There still is no dishwasher at Fairway Ranch, and my sweetheart kept his promise. Even more than that, he thanked me for every breakfast, lunch, and dinner. For my part, it took fourteen years for me to realize I should be thanking him for doing the dishes. Yet when I would thank him, he would say, "You don't need to thank me for that, sweetheart—there's so little I can do for you." Indeed.

What struck me the most about Uncle Byron was his devotion to others. He was smitten with Auntie Weese [Louise] for more than fifty years, and he was smitten with Aunt Peggy for almost twenty. He was the perfect example of a devoted, loyal, and loving spouse who knew how to adore and really truly love each of his wives. He was devoted first to God, then to his spouse, then to his family, and then to golf. Whatever he was involved in, he put his whole heart into.

Nicole Mitchell Youngblood
Byron's Great-Niece

Hale and Hearty

Byron felt I might have some concern about his general health at nearly seventy-five, so he had a thorough physical examination and even assured me that he had all his teeth. When I said, half-joking, that if he didn't I might not be so sure about all this, he answered, "I wouldn't blame you." How's that for being understanding?

Byron even felt a charming obligation to meet my mother and let her know his "intentions." Since she lived in Toledo, and the PGA Championship was being held there that year at his old club, Inverness, it worked out well for us to meet there and enjoy some time at the tournament. I also had some fun getting to play golf for the first time with my big brother, Ed, and telling him of my impending plans.

As we were on the way to his course, I said I was getting married again, and he asked, "Who to?"

I replied, "Byron Nelson."

Ed laughed, then looked at me and said, "You're not kidding, are you?"

I said, "No, I'm not."

He got pretty quiet for the rest of the ride, and I have to say I don't think the news really helped his game much that day, although I was having a great time.

Years later, though, Ed reflected, "Byron was great to talk to about golf. And he was good for my sister." What a great brother!

In the summer of 1986, Joe and I were at President Ford's tournament in Vail, Colorado. I invited Byron to stay with us, since Louise had died, and he did. Every night we were there, Byron would ask Joe if we could drive by the post office on our way to the parties so he could mail his special lady a letter. Then when we were at the party, he'd be looking at his watch every ten minutes like a sixteen-year-old smitten with the love bug. He'd ask what time we were leaving, and I'd say, "Well, Joe's tired, so we can leave now." He wanted to get home and make his phone call, since Ohio was two hours ahead, and he wanted that "goodnight kiss." Too cute!

Barbara and Joe Kern
Friends since 1980

5

Texas Tee Off

By the end of August 1986, plans were underway for me to move to Texas lock, stock, and barrel. So on September 7, I picked up Byron at the airport one more time, and we loaded the car. By then I had bought a nifty secondhand black Lincoln Continental, quite an upgrade from my orange Ford Pinto of five years before. We packed it with such worldly goods as I thought would be appropriate for a cattle rancher/golfer's wife-to-be, which was mostly clothes and makeup. After all, I knew his home had to be filled with beautiful furniture, art, and antiques, and I certainly didn't have anything to contribute to that. We planned to ship my piano later.

So we were on the road, down through Kentucky, Tennessee, and Arkansas. I remember doing some pretty deep thinking as we drove along. (Byron drove the entire distance, by the way.) After all, this was a pretty extraordinary place to which I had come. Reflecting on my past failures in life, lack of direction or career, or anything remotely resembling the fairy-tale existence I had pictured as a child, I vowed with all my heart, whispering to myself, *Whatever it takes, Lord, this is going to work.* Little did I know even then that it was going to be 90 percent Byron, with me just trying to catch up all the time. But at least I was determined to do my best.

Stopping the first night in Jackson, Tennessee, we got to enjoy the local tourist attraction: railroad's Casey Jones of song and legend. Byron also got a chuckle out of the reaction of the desk clerk at the hotel when he said he wanted two rooms for two people, his fiancée and him. She was dumbfounded. Guess she just didn't know about Christian folks from Texas.

Late the next afternoon we pulled into the Chaparral apartment complex in Irving, Texas. I was ushered into a beautifully furnished one-bedroom place and found a delicious lemon poppyseed cake waiting for us from Byron's dear friends, Steve and Shaun Barley. Even more wonderful was a lovely Lenox porcelain collector's plate. On the front was a painting of a Revolutionary War soldier whispering in the ear of his exquisitely gowned sweetheart. Byron asked me to turn the plate over, and my heart was caught up again at the title, "The Unexpected Proposal." Mr. Romance, as I was to realize again and again, could have been Byron's middle name. And that plate still has a place of honor in our home. I was safely installed in the apartment for the night, while Byron drove twenty miles west to the ranch.

Fairway Ranch

The next morning, Byron picked me up at the apartment and brought me out to Fairway Ranch for the first time. As he made the left turn onto what was then Litsey Road (later renamed Eleven Straight Lane in honor of his 1945 streak), he pointed out the five-foot-high rock fence corner that marked the southeast boundary of his front pasture. On the front of the rock face were the words "Byron Nelson's Fairway Ranch" in wrought iron. I thought it was classy and certainly showed his satisfaction in achieving his long-ago dream. The French light on top of the wall, he said, had been installed shortly after he and Louise bought the ranch, and it was a great help in guiding people onto the road after dark, both for them and their neighbors.

About an eighth of a mile along the road, he turned right into a long driveway, and that was when I first could really see the house, surrounded by about a dozen trees—red oaks, live oaks, and two huge hackberries that sheltered the very front. Though it's large—4,400 square feet and much bigger than anywhere I had lived before—I immediately felt very much at home, because it is a comfortable kind of place, not intimidating at all. It's warm and friendly and welcoming, like Byron himself.

Built in 1938, the original house has been expanded and re-modeled through the years, as Byron and Louise worked with a great architect and wonderful skilled helpers to transform what had been a fairly ordinary ranch house into a place where they could graciously entertain family, friends, and pro golfers. It was the only home they ever really lived in and owned just for themselves, and for Louise, it was a dream come true.

After showing me through the house, Byron took me on a driving tour around the ranch, which was a pie-wedge shaped piece of property, about 750 acres at the time. With Hereford cattle and some crossbred cows dotting the hillsides, it was a whole lot of wide-open spaces for this city girl.

During the tour, Byron pointed out the two large barns used for storing hay and ranch equipment, then the three houses nearby. Across the road his ranch manager, Eddie Baggs, lived with his wife, Marcia, and their two little girls, Maeci and Erin. Down the road, in a house Byron built for his parents in the 1950s, lived Bruce and Donna Steele and their daughter, Tara. Directly across the driveway from him lived his sister and her husband, Ellen and Farish Sherman.

Then he drove me down to the lake to see the cabin, which he and Louise had crafted in the 1960s when they first began remodeling the main house. Those original kitchen cabinets and much of the paneling now in the cabin are still there, and it was used through the years as extra living space for temporary ranch helpers. Today we have updated it a bit and made it into a very pleasant small guest house.

The last stop on the tour was Byron's woodshop, where he created his many gifts, large and small, for friends and family. It was great fun to see how proud he was of the equipment he had and how much pleasure he gained from this absorbing hobby.

Oh, and I also got to meet Byron's Rhode Island Red chickens and took advantage of the opportunity to do my chicken imitation, which probably impressed him about as much as my golf swing. After all, my maiden name *is* McDonald, so I had that much going for me as a prospective farmer's wife. Byron had liked chickens ever since he was a little fellow. "Chickens talk to you," he'd say. He had even won a blue ribbon with one of them when he was a kid at the local county fair.

Riding Tall in the Saddle

I've heard many stories about Byron and the ranch through the years from family and friends. His nephew David Nelson told me this one:

> As a young child, I had the opportunity to spend a lot of time at the ranch, because my parents, Charles and Betty Nelson, worked at Camp Sweeney in Gainesville in the summer. Since we lived in the Rio Grande Valley, we visited the ranch on the day and a half we had off each week. We would stay at Grandmother Nelson's house, arriving Thursday and leaving early Sunday morning when we would drive back to camp. All of this occurred during my cowboy phase. My heroes at the time all rode horses and chased bad guys. Roy Rogers, Gene Autry, *The Lone Ranger*, *Wagon Train*, and *Bonanza* were all shows I watched and whose characters I became at play.
>
> When I was at the ranch, my grandfather, Daddy John, and Uncle Byron became Ben Cartwright and Rowdy Yates. I know they were just taking care of the cattle while on horseback, but in

my mind they were protecting the herd from the band of rustlers who were camped just over the ridge from the lake house.

So when I hear "Byron Nelson," the first picture that comes to mind is not the young golfer with the great swing or of him and Chris Schenkel in the broadcast booth or him greeting the players at the Four Seasons. It's of him and Daddy John riding tall in the saddle on Linda and Red, heading down the hill from the corrals to set the world straight, with Grandmother Nelson and me following behind in the old Ford pickup.

All the superlatives have already been written about my uncle so I won't try to repeat them here. As I grew older, he went from being my cowboy uncle to a celebrity athlete whom the world loved and admired. I appreciated and admired all that as well, but to me, he was just my dad's big brother and the most rock-solid guy in the world.

Facing the Family

Then it was time to meet the family, or families. I can no longer recall in what order this all happened, but I believe first was the meeting with Louise's younger sister, Kathleen, and her husband, Howard Morell. Sadly, Howard was in the last stages of emphysema at the time, but he welcomed me so sweetly as I entered the living room of their home in Fort Worth.

"Welcome to Texas, Peggy!" he called out from his chair, and it felt so good.

I guess I should have been more worried about how Louise's family would feel, but Byron had assured me that he thought everything would be just fine. I learned later that he had prepared not only Louise's family but also his own family and even some of the folks at his church that this Yankee was a-comin'.

The visit with shy Kathleen and Howard went smoothly. Next was a trip to Dallas to meet Mike and Eunice Massad. Mike had been chairman of the Byron Nelson tournament in 1978. In fact, he was one of the team who came to Byron in 1967 to ask for permission to use his name on the event to improve the field. When we walked into their living room, Byron and Mike began talking golf, while beautiful, blue-eyed Eunice and I soon found a mutual love for writing and English literature and had a merry conversation. Another hurdle crossed. So far I seemed to be doing okay.

Lord Byron and the Bible

The following Sunday, Byron picked me up and we went to church in Roanoke. Then we met for lunch at nearby Trophy Club Country Club with his brother, Charles, and his wife, Betty; plus his sister, Ellen, and her husband, Farish. I imagine they were closely checking me out at several levels, but I was honestly so very in love with Byron that I was not concerned with their reaction to me as much as I wanted to please Byron and make him proud.

In the meantime, Byron had been helping me learn more about the Bible. Having already visited a Church of Christ in Dayton at Byron's suggestion, I was open to this new way of thinking, using the Bible as the main focus for doctrine and understanding about God.

And because I had previously taken several classes on the Psalms, the gospel of Mark, and even Greek, I guess you could say I was primed for accepting what Byron was teaching me.

Having grown up in the Catholic church and then leaving it, I had also rejected any connection with organized religion for more than fifteen years. But shortly after I first met Byron in 1981, I felt a strong need to get back to God and had been going to church in Dayton for several years before coming to Texas. I already believed in Jesus as the Son of God and in the Trinity, so moving into the Church of Christ wasn't a huge leap of faith or struggle for me—how could it be with Byron guiding me on this new pathway? Most of what he was teaching me was familiar by now, and it was not long before I

One of my first encounters with Byron was in the spring of 1982, shortly after I became the executive director of the Salesmanship Club of Dallas, sponsor of Byron's Championship since 1968. For years after that I watched Byron interact with players, patrons, spectators, Club members, and staff. He was the same with each of us—thoughtful, considerate, gentle, and genuine. Byron was conscientious about sending notes or calling after the tournament, complimenting the staff for a job well done, and letting us know he appreciated our work on his behalf. Simply acknowledging our efforts made all the long days more than worthwhile. Despite his celebrity status, he took time to make us feel special in our roles. His example inspired us to try our best to treat others with respect and consideration too.

Janie Henderson
Executive Director
Salesmanship Club, 1990–2008

realized I needed to do just as the Bible said and be baptized. So on October 19, about a month before our wedding, Byron baptized me into the Lord before the entire congregation—our spiritual family. That date is even more important in my mind than our wedding day. Plus, can you imagine being baptized by Lord Byron? How's that for something to live up to! I still remember Howard Morell's phone call that evening:

"Hello, Sister Peggy. Congratulations!"

True Texas Women

Next on the list of people to meet were Louise's nieces—Sandy Mitchell and Carla and Delane Newell—quite an imposing phalanx of very well-dressed and coiffed true Texas women. We met for lunch in Fort Worth with me dressed in a skirt and sweater, still having no clue that whenever you went anywhere in Texas, you had better be dressed up. But they were all very kind to me, and later I realized that as much as they had all loved Louise and missed her, they also had been very worried about Byron as he lost weight and even the will to live since the love of his life had died. So they were willing to give me a chance, as Byron had asked them to do before he even brought me to Texas. Later Sandy called him and said something like, "Well, I think when she gets fixed up a little bit, she'll do just fine!"

It didn't take long for that transformation to begin. The next week Byron took me to Lester Melnick's, a wonderful store in Highland Park, where I had my own saleswoman and just the right amount of personal attention. In fact, the buyer made a special trip to New York to select the perfect wedding dress. It was absolutely exquisite—a pale peach champagne color with long lace sleeves and lace inset down the back, a dropped waist, and tea-length skirt. There was even a matching silk bow for my hair, which at the time was nearly shoulder-length. Truly the dress made me feel like a princess. I still have it and sometimes I can almost fit into it.

6

One Wonderful Wedding Day

Planning for the wedding and the wedding day was a dreamlike experience for me. We sent more than one hundred invitations and a hundred more announcements.

Our friends Barbara and Joe Kern gave us a lovely engagement party about a month before the wedding, and it was nearly as special as the wedding itself. About fifty of Byron's closest Dallas friends from the Salesmanship Club and Preston Trail were there to meet me and see just exactly what sort of Yankee Byron had brought to Texas. I remember making a promise to everyone there, the two of us standing on the staircase landing just above the living room in their amazing home, that I would take good care of Byron and love him with all my heart. If only they had known how easy that was to do!

The Four Seasons folks were eager to do whatever they could for Byron—everyone was so delighted to see him happy again after all he had been through. Then his friends from the Salesmanship Club put together a wonderful tour of Dallas for my family when they arrived the day before the wedding. We had lunch at the historic and impressive Neiman-Marcus flagship store in downtown Dallas, toured the exquisite neighborhoods in Highland Park, and finished by driving to Valley Ranch in time to see the Dallas Cowboys come off the practice field and meet legendary coach Tom Landry.

On our actual wedding day, my family came to the ranch, and I made lunch—lasagna, salad, garlic bread, and dessert. What made it remarkable was that the power went off for about an hour that morning (something I was soon to find was not an unusual occurrence for us country folk), which made the lunch timing hectic. But everyone certainly got enough to eat, and while we were enjoying the dessert, suddenly there appeared next to my plate a small package, beautifully wrapped. My oldest brother, Ed, who was the most avid golfer of my siblings, had placed it there.

I said, "How'd that get there?"

Ed replied, "I think Byron used a wedge."

Opening it I discovered a beautiful gold watch by Cyma, which I continue to wear for almost every special occasion.

Then it was my turn, and I presented Lord Byron with a pair of gold cufflinks bearing inset sapphires and his initials. He was pleased and always proud to wear them. Plus, on our second anniversary or thereabouts, Byron overwhelmed me with a diamond dinner ring set with thirty-two diamonds, while I stunned him with a Cyma men's watch to match the one he'd given me. We surely did love giving gifts, both small and large, to each other—and he was always so appreciative that it encouraged me to do it more often.

A Small Worry at the Wedding

You can't really tell from the wedding pictures, but my tea-length dress was fastened in the back with just three hooks and eyes—at the neck, midback, and waist. During the fitting process it never caused a problem, but when time came for the ceremony, that middle hook would *not* stay hooked, and my heart quailed at the thought of its coming undone in front of a hundred of Byron's closest friends and our families. So I sent my son John to find a pair of pliers, which he borrowed from our photographer, Brad Bradley, and John squeezed that hook closed to within an inch of its life.

Then it was time for my two handsome young sons to walk me down the aisle and hand me over to Byron. One delightful note about the ceremony itself: Byron had told me well ahead of time that at most weddings the guests could barely hear anything the bride and groom said, so he was going to say his vows loud and clear. When he did, his "I do!" boomed out in our tiny auditorium and surprised the preacher, C. N. Taylor, to such an extent that he joined in with a loud "Amen!" and the whole church laughed out loud, including me.

Back to that hook-and-eye situation: John did such a great job that, when we finally arrived at our hotel room after the reception, Byron had to use quite a bit of his famed perseverance to pry that thing apart, or I might have just had to wear that dress for a very long time!

Happily Ever After

As for our honeymoon, it wasn't Hawaii or Europe or even Canada or Mexico. Instead we chose to drive to Kerrville and stay at Byron's vacation home at Riverhill Country Club on the tenth fairway of the golf course he and Joe Finger had designed for Sherman and Stuart Hunt back in 1974. It's a charming place and made the perfect honeymoon/golf getaway. However, when Louise's sister Kathleen Morell called on Tuesday morning to tell us that Howard, her beloved husband of forty years—the man who had welcomed me to Texas only two months earlier—had passed away, we just packed up, came back home, and life moved on. But it was indeed a sweet, dear time for us to get better acquainted and spend actual days and nights together at last.

We were so delighted with each other and having such grand times right off that it won't surprise anyone to know we celebrated everything we could think of in those first few weeks. In fact on December 15, just one month after our wedding, I made a special dinner for us at home. As we sat at our beautiful dining room table and opened the "anniversary" cards we had chosen for each other, Byron announced, "I want to celebrate our anniversary every month, sweetheart, because I'll never have enough time with you." What a dear man! And so we did all through the months and years that the good Lord gave us.

For a while Byron was a little concerned that I might regret getting married so quickly and want to go back to Ohio. It never occurred to me, honestly. After all, with both of my sons away at college by

I saw Byron cry only once, and I cried with him. We were together at the resort in a quiet setting at the Byron Nelson Golf School. We had held a small birthday celebration for him among the golf staff. He was starting to have more difficulty with his mobility and these types of celebrations were becoming more rare. The room had cleared, it was time to go, so he asked me to find a phone so he could call Peggy and tell her he was on his way home. (It was an understanding they had so that neither worried too much about the other driving between town and the ranch in Roanoke.) After speaking to her, he turned to me and told me how much he loved her and how badly he felt for the difficulties he felt she had endured through helping nurse him back to health after his recent second hip operation. He wept unabashedly and said they would never have enough time on earth together. I thought the world would be a better place if every couple could share that kind of love.

Angela Enright
Public Relations Director,
Four Seasons Resort and Club

then, there was really no reason to go back. Besides I was learning on a daily basis that this Mr. Nelson was full of all kinds of delightful surprises, and apparently he thought I was the cat's pajamas too. It was an exhilarating and novel feeling for me, and I fully intended to do my part to make sure it stayed that way.

Did we ever have conflicts? Of course, but mostly the conflict was on my side and in my mind, and there was a huge difference in the outcome from anything I had ever experienced before, because of the way Byron handled the situation. I still remember the first time I got upset with him, about a month after we were married. We were in the kitchen cleaning up after supper, and he said something that bothered me. I became very quiet, which was better than saying what

I was thinking at the time, but it didn't take even two minutes for Byron to realize something was wrong. He put down the dishtowel, walked out of the room for a few minutes, and then came back in.

"Sweetheart," he said, "it distresses me so to know I've upset you. Please tell me what I can do to make it right."

I just stood there, open-mouthed in amazement. I had never heard anyone say anything like that in my life—not my parents, not even folks in romantic movies or fairy tales. It took a few more minutes for me to marshal my scattered thoughts and say what had bothered me, and of course, within a few weeks, I couldn't even remember it myself.

It proved always to be true that if I got upset about something, Byron was even more upset that he had upset me. And that insight helped me to grow much more compassionate, understanding, and forgiving (most of the time) than was my nature. I actually would have the last word in all of these situations, though, because I got to say, "I'm sorry I got upset." That was good, because most of the time my fussing wasn't over anything worthwhile. And I even grew up enough to ask him to forgive me, to which Byron would inevitably reply, "There's nothing to forgive." Is that not amazing?

In fact, Byron was so totally understanding of my relative immaturity, and recognized his own imperfections to such a degree, that sometimes he would say, "I wish you'd get upset with me more often—I'd feel better then." I told him that wasn't really a good idea. When I finally matured enough to bring up a problem before I got to the boiling point, he would sit very quietly and listen to what I had to say, and then, more often than not, he answered, "I've been told that before." That actually made me feel better, knowing that Louise had perhaps been bothered by the same thing in the past, and since she was such a wonderful person, maybe I wasn't too far off myself. Then he would always follow with, "And I promise to try never to do it again." Wouldn't marriages do much better today if we could all follow that simple, heartfelt example?

7

Moving to Fairway Ranch

You may wonder if it was difficult for me to move into this home that Byron and Louise had lived in and loved for more than forty years. It took me a while to realize that, especially for Louise, this was the only true home she and Byron ever had. Although in 1940 they had bought a fifty-four-acre farm and house in Denton, Texas, they shared it with Byron's parents and his brother and sister while the two younger siblings went through college and into their own marriages. However, since 1940–46 were Byron's most important years on the tour, particularly 1944–45, he and Louise really didn't spent very much time at the Denton farm anyway. Often in the winter months they were in Texarkana with Louise's family or on the road.

Byron prepared me for Fairway Ranch just the same sweet way he had prepared family and friends for me. During one of our phone conversations after our engagement, he said, "I want you to know that when we're married, you will be the queen of this house, and whatever you want to do, within reason, we'll do." He more than kept his word on that, calling one day to say that he had taken down all of the pictures of Louise and either given them to her family or stored them away. He even asked if it would be all right if we kept one out. It was his favorite picture of the two of them, taken on the front steps of Milton Hershey's home (yes, *that* Mr. Hershey) in 1940 after Byron had won the PGA championship at Hershey Country Club in 1940. It's a lovely hand-tinted photograph, and of course I said yes.

Byron truly loved Louise with all his heart, and he spoke tenderly of her many great qualities as wife, cook, homemaker, and supporter of all his endeavors. He also spoke a number of times of regrets that he had about being so focused on golf that at times he wasn't as considerate of her needs as he might have been. But they were a great team, and that was probably the one thing that worried me about how I would fit into this new partnership. I had never had the experience of being on any kind of team, athletic or otherwise, and being an independent woman, I wasn't sure I could really live up to that standard. But I was determined to make it, and with Byron's and the Lord's help, I somehow managed it . . . most of the time.

Daily Life on the Ranch

Life passed peacefully on the ranch day to day, sprinkled with the excitement of golf tournaments, travel, celebrity events, and other activities we both enjoyed. One of the things about Byron that impressed me so much was his relationship with the wonderful people who work on the ranch. One of those folks is Eddie Baggs, who lives on the ranch and is also a Texas AgriLife Extension Service Agent, so he has an enormous amount of valuable information about ranching. Eddie told me this story:

When I came to work for Byron in 1981, I was a rodeo cowboy and bull rider, never played golf and had no interest in it at all, so I'd hardly even heard his name. In fact, when I first met him out in his woodshop, he was dressed in a short-sleeved khaki shirt and khaki pants and old shoes, and he looked like just an old farmer.

When I'd been at the ranch a couple of months, he asked if I played golf, and I told him I'd never swung a club and had no interest in it.

He said, "Well, if you're going to live and work out here, you might have to learn."

I said I'd rather not; I'd rather just feed cattle and build fences, and he replied that he'd appreciate it if I'd give it a try. So he handed me an old Wilson blade nine-iron, which I found out later were about the hardest clubs to hit ever made, and a paper sack one-third full of golf balls. He told me to just hit a few balls whenever I had some free time, and not to worry about picking them up, but when I got to where I could hit three in a row solid (never mind where they went) to come back to him.

Since I didn't yet know who he really was and was completely uninterested, it took several months before I could honestly tell Mr. Nelson that I'd done it. In fact, I mostly used that nine-iron to push cattle around! But when I was able to tell him I'd hit three in a row and used up all the balls in that sack, he watched me swing and said, "Can I show you one thing?" And he gave me my first lesson, showing me the right way to grip the club. Then he gave me another paper sack, more golf balls, an eight-iron, and eventually another tip on where to place the ball in my stance.

Several more months went by, and then there were more balls, a seven, then six, then five-iron and more short lessons, till finally I had a fairly good swing and a whole set of these Wilson irons. This all took about two whole years, to show you how reluctant I was, though somewhere along the way I did finally figure out who this Mr. Nelson really was.

When I started to school at Texas A&M, I did it while still working at the ranch on weekends and between semesters. One of the degree requirements was a physical education class, and one of the options was golf, so I chose that one. I'd still never played on a golf course of any kind, and A&M had a pretty good one where I could play for free, so I began to play there. One day the golf coach saw me on the practice range, said I had a good swing, and wanted to know who taught me. When I told him "Byron Nelson," he didn't believe me at first, but I managed to convince him eventually.

By this time I was getting pretty interested in the game, and Byron told me that when I could bring him a scorecard showing I'd broken ninety, we'd go play together. Now I became obsessed, playing any time I could, even cutting classes and kind of neglecting my family, which now included two little girls. But finally I shot an eighty-eight, brought the card to Byron, and he set it up for us to go play at Preston Trail in Dallas, where his tournament had been held the first fifteen years. As it turned out there was quite a nice gallery that came to see this exhibition. I was extremely nervous and didn't play worth a lick, but I was as high as a kite anyway. I wish I could tell you I became a scratch or even a single-digit handicap golfer, but I do love the game now.

In the process Byron taught me a lot about faith, humility, conservation—and yes, even golf—that have been great blessings to my life. Most importantly Byron brought me to see, know, and love God, eventually baptizing my whole family, and that means the world to me.

Byron loved helping and encouraging other people in whatever area they needed it, and just as with Eddie, the results often had eternal benefits.

Spiffing Up Our Castle

It made such an enormous difference that Byron did everything he could to make me feel comfortable, and as beautifully as the house had been decorated through the years, it took me quite a while to work up the courage to make even a suggestion for change. It had to be that the wallpaper was literally coming off the guest room walls, or the dining room window treatment was looking awfully tired after thirty years' service. Even then, as I pored over fabrics and wall coverings, I would mentally ask Louise if she preferred this one or that one. Byron proved a great help in this area, because he had a good eye for color and pattern and kept me from making some fairly egregious errors.

Not only did he have a good fashion sense, he had a lot of practical wisdom. When I was deciding on fabric for the drapes for the dining room picture window, I had narrowed down the selection to three patterns, ranging in price from $29 to $64 per square yard. I liked all three but wanted some help in making a final choice, so I called in Lord Byron, my best fashion consultant.

He examined all three samples, looked up at the window and at the sketch from our designer, then he told me,

Now sweetheart, I've been married a long time, and I've learned a few things. All three of these fabrics are beautiful, and I'll be happy with whichever one you like best. But if you really like the most expensive one, you'd better get that, because if you don't, five years or so down the road you're going to want to change it out, and you'll end up spending more money than if you'd gotten what you wanted in the first place.

That's a remarkable enough thing for any husband to say, but please be sure to notice something very special about it: Byron could have said that *he* would be spending all that money, which of course was true in any case, but he never looked at it that way. I think he trusted in my basic judgment that I wouldn't "go haywire," as we say in Texas. He also figured that I was just enough intimidated by the whole situation that I wouldn't go off the deep end. But with his words ringing in my ears, I did go with the most expensive of the three, and that window treatment is just the same fifteen years later. I still love it, and as far as I'm concerned, it will be there when I go to heaven myself, even if that's thirty years from now. So you see Mr. Wonderful was Mr. Right in more ways than one!

Probably the biggest change we made was in the formal living room, which had been decorated very tastefully by Louise many years before. The carpet and several chairs were a pale gray-blue, and the drapes and two loveseats that faced each other by the fireplace sported a handsome oriental print on a cream background. The overall effect was very cool and calm. However, over the first five years or so of our marriage, I noticed that when we had company, no one ever went in that room to visit or eat unless there wasn't enough seating space elsewhere. It occurred to me that the coolness of the décor might not be very welcoming. So I wanted to lighten and warm it up with off-white carpet and some brighter colors on the furniture, which needed to be replaced by then anyway. Byron gave me a budget to include carpet, furniture, and drapes, and when I came in under that amount, he decided I could do no wrong! Pretty funny. But as it turned out, the room is a lovely, warm, inviting place now, and even though we did less entertaining over the last five years of our marriage, for sure it's a lot more welcoming, light, and colorful than it was before.

Dressing the Part

With Byron's excellent help and Edna Palmer's assistance at Lester Melnick's, I soon acquired a wardrobe suitable for our travels and all sorts of social doings. I was to find out that Edna was worth her weight

I remember the first day I met Byron. Peggy had invited Cheree and me over for lunch with Marcia and Eddie Baggs and Jim and Mary Ann Izzarelli. We were all in the dining room, admiring the decorations and getting acquainted. I think everyone intentionally left the seat right next to me for Byron, who hadn't come in yet.

When he did come in, he stopped, looked directly at me, and said, "Hello, I'm Byron," as if I wouldn't know who he was. As we shook hands, his completely enveloped mine, so much that I was shocked, not only at the size but at the strength. It was kind of an out-of-body experience for me, one handshake I'll always remember.

As we enjoyed the meal and dinner conversation, I was amazed at how Byron didn't struggle to mix with the group. He didn't seem to know we were in the presence of a celebrity, "Byron Nelson the golfer." He was simply Byron the man.

Tim Johnson
Fairway Ranch Neighbor and Friend

in gold, because once I went shopping for a trip we were about to take, and Edna wasn't there that day. Another lady helped me, one of those commission-conscious folks who kept saying, "Oh, that's a perfect color for you!" and "You've just *got* to have that dress," and so on.

The upshot of it was that her flattery turned my silly head, and I came home with not one or two but eight outfits, and as I modeled them for Byron, I noticed his growing lack of enthusiasm. He didn't say anything, but I realized I had gone over the top, so the next day I took all but one purchase back to the store. They were not very happy about that, of course. I only kept the one to remind myself of my foolishness and only wore that one twice. He told me later he didn't care how much I bought as long as I actually wore the clothes, but he hadn't thought any of those dresses and suits were flattering to me. Another lesson learned.

Making Someone's Day Better

Andy McConnell, who is the farrier at the ranch and our friend, remembers Byron saying, "If we can make one person's day better because we are in it, then we have done something wonderful." He also told me this story about an encounter he had with Byron on the ranch:

One day I was on the farm alone (not a big deal), but for some reason I was in a very foul mood because of it. It was very hot that day, and I had shod many horses that week for other customers, including putting all the horses back in their pastures after they were shod or trimmed. As I pulled out through the gate at the Nelsons' barn, I was hot, exhausted, and still in a mood much like that of a cornered badger. I saw Byron's minivan pulling into his driveway, and I got back in my truck because I couldn't be bothered talking to anyone right then. As I started down the road, Byron flagged me down.

Oh, great, what next! I thought. Reluctantly I rolled down the window.

"Hi, Andy," he said. "How are you?"

"I'm okay, Mr. Nelson," I answered.

Byron said, "You look tired. You need to take care of yourself in this hot sun."

"Yes, sir,"

"I'm sorry I wasn't around to visit, Andy," he continued. "We've been busy working on my tournament. But I promise that I will come see you next time. Peggy and I really appreciate what you do. And we always enjoy seeing you. So have a good day and get some rest."

I think I got out a barely audible, "Yes sir."

As Byron drove off, I sat there for a moment. I felt like a selfish jerk, not that Byron would have wanted that reaction. I also got a little choked up, because no matter how small a role you may have played in Byron's life, when you were there, you felt very important.

Now I try to always take time for people when I see someone down in the dumps and give them a little light. Byron had a certain energy about him, and I hope that someday I can be half the person he was. But I figured out that day that the little things do count. And as they say, a journey of a thousand miles begins with a single step. We can make a change with little things. I think Byron would be glad to know that the lesson of making just one person's day better by seeing us left an indelible mark.

My life has become wonderful, and Byron helped me with his little bits through the hard times. I wish I could share with him how cool things are now and how special a person he was in my little world. I try to impact at least one person every day. I think Byron would like it that way.

You may think Andy's story is unique, but it's similar to dozens of stories about Byron's interactions with folks that I've heard through the years. It was his "normal."

8

The Great Piano Saga

The one large item I brought from Ohio to Texas was my piano—a small console by Story & Clark, which we had shipped shortly after the wedding and placed in the living room. Now I had time to play and practice, and I began to work on it as best I could. Two things stopped me from progressing much: I didn't have a teacher, and I realized that I didn't really like that piano—its tone, its sound. Maybe because it was now living in this beautiful home, it just wasn't up to par with its new surroundings.

I don't know that I would ever have done anything about it, but Byron so loved hearing me play the few pieces I could that I came up with a proposal and presented it to him. I asked him if I were to commit to taking lessons and practicing faithfully for at least two years, could we upgrade to a better piano? He kindly agreed, so I searched and found first a teacher, Lil Teddlie. She was a friend of

Life with Lord Byron

Byron's brother Charles's accompanist, Jean Mainous, and Lil proved a complete delight.

Speaking of Byron's brother, Charles, you should know that he is an internationally well-known baritone. He is as gifted musically as Byron was in golf, having sung in major venues worldwide. He is a consumate performer and conductor, serving as Artist in Residence at Abilene Christian University (ACU) for eleven years. He now serves ACU as Professor Emeritus of Music. Perhaps that's one reason Byron enjoyed music. And Charles has some wonderful memories of growing up with Byron:

> When the third child arrived in the Nelson household, according to family lore, six-foot-two, fourteen-year-old Byron assumed many new chores enthusiastically and without complaint, including diaper changing. He gave the baby a lot of personal attention. And naturally, infants bond quickly to those who give them attention. He was always aware and considerate. He always picked me up when he came home in the afternoon. He never minded a little brother tagging along to the golf course as he stole putting practice on a secluded green at dusk. He played games with me in the evening. He even taught me to count and play dominoes. He was my hero, and I adored him. During the day, when I would misbehave, all mother had to say was, "I'm going to tell your brother," and I was back on the straight and narrow.
>
> I was seven when Byron married Louise. A week after their honeymoon, he had me sent, by train, from Fort Worth to Texarkana to spend a week with them. To me it seemed a normal

course of events. In retrospect, it's astonishing. I would bend over backwards to do anything he asked of me. He never asked much. However, when my hero, my strongest role model, was always firm, courteous, considerate, truthful, honest, and just, along with being a world-class master of his craft, it made me reach and stretch and strain to become the best I could become. At no time, during the eighty years of our life as brothers, did he ever disappoint me. He remains my hero and role model.

Charles went on to say,

I was judging a choral contest with the renowned professional choral director, Roger Wagner. If you're not into choral music, you might not know of him, but he was considered the second best (behind Robert Shaw) choral director in the country. Roger had been told I was Byron's brother.

During the several days we spent together, he said, "I almost played golf with your brother once."

"Oh really?" I replied. "How did that happen?"

"Well," he said, "I was playing in California, and I was playing alone. I played up on the threesome ahead of me. One of them asked if I would like to join them, and I did. Before I got to hit my ball, my caddie asked if I knew who that man was. I said I didn't recognize him."

He said, "That's Byron Nelson."

I excused myself and went back to the club house. I wasn't going to hit a ball in the presence of Byron Nelson!

Then Charles laughed and said, "My good friend Jim Campbell retired from being principal of Gainesville High School and director of Camp Sweeney, and he moved to Waco, Texas, to be near his son. With nothing to do, one Saturday morning he decided to go to a dog show, which was being held at the fairgrounds. Walking through the maze of show dogs, he saw an unfamiliar breed and stopped to talk to the owner. The conversation went something like this:

Jim: 'That's a good-looking dog you have there. I don't recognize the breed.'

Owner: 'It's a British breed. There are not many of them in this country.'

Jim: 'I guess it is worth a lot of money.'

Owner: 'As a pup he cost me twelve hundred dollars and an airline ticket from London to the United States.'

Jim: 'Does the dog have a name?'

Owner: 'His name is Byron Nelson.'

Jim: (Jim had met Byron on a number of occasions.) 'That's a little unusual. How did you come to choose that name?'

Owner: 'I was attending the Byron Nelson Golf Classic. I got tired and sat down on a bench in the shade of a tree. Byron Nelson walked up and sat on the bench with me. He talked to me just as if I were as important as those pros who were playing in the tournament. That's why I named my prized possession Byron Nelson.'"

But back to my own musical journey. After finding Lil, I drove to Fort Worth and encountered the amazing McBrayer Piano Gallery, which had a beautiful Steinway console from 1947. A Steinway, for goodness' sake! We gave my old Story & Clark to Eddie and Marcia, whose girls were old enough by then to begin lessons of their own, and the Steinway came to live at the ranch while I began to learn the intricacies of scales, Hanon's exercises, and dozens of other mysteries Lil tried hard to teach me.

Our piano buying didn't stop with that small Steinway, though. Now that we were making regular one-week trips each month to Kerrville, it just wouldn't do for me to miss all those days of practice (I say this with full knowledge that I wasn't really practicing all that much at home, but I surely meant to!). So at first I tried to use the piano at the clubhouse in the afternoons, but that wasn't very satisfactory. Then we trekked to San Antonio, over an hour's drive away, and bought a Hamilton studio model—not pretty, but it had a good sound and feel. So now I was without excuse, as the Bible would say, and did actually practice several days on those trips, more for Byron's enjoyment than from any burning dedication on my part.

The next step came when I spied an absolutely gorgeous antique Kranich & Bach upright at a local antique mall in Kerrville. It was so lovely and would fit nicely in our home there. Happily, Sharon Edson Williams, the daughter of Byron's woodworking friend Harris Edson, had been thinking of getting a piano and playing on her own. So we worked out a deal with her, and eventually we had a fabulous piece of furniture that could make pretty good music, Sharon had her own instrument to play, and everyone was happy.

Ah, but the saga continues. My good friend back home, Maryann Izzarelli, who had taken seven years of lessons as a child, became infected by all my piano talk and began longing to get one herself. I took her to McBrayer's to find one, and while she was discussing with Monte McBrayer about ways and means, I wandered around the store checking out the various brands and styles, knowing my sweet Steinway at home was just too wonderful for words.

The Piano Shuffle

Then it happened. Over in the grand piano department, I saw from the back a deep walnut grand piano, a wonderful chocolate brown finish with rich grain and warm reddish highlights. Of course I had never thought of having a grand myself, because I didn't consider my level of inexpertise worth it. I certainly was intrigued by the finish on this one, though, because I didn't care for the highly lacquered and polished black ones I had seen elsewhere. As I strolled around to the keyboard side, I saw again that magic name, Steinway & Sons. Then I made the fatal mistake of striking just one key. I think it was E above middle C. And oh! What a full, rich, sweet tone it had.

Maryann had finished her conversation with Monte, so we drove home a few minutes later. She decided that it was too much money and she didn't have the right to ask Jim to spend that much when she wasn't finished with her real estate studies.

That evening I told Byron about our adventures, and when I recounted the magic of the tone of that Steinway at the store, Byron rubbed his chin thoughtfully for a minute and said, "I'd like to see that piano, sweetheart."

The next day we had an appointment in Dallas and decided to go home by way of Fort Worth and McBrayer's. So I sat down and played just a few chords and a song or two on that wonderful instrument, and Byron said, "Honey, if I thought we had room for it, I'd buy that piano for you right now."

We expressed our dilemma to Monte, who solved it by loaning us a template—a piece of substantial vinyl fabric in the shape of a grand piano and adjustable to whichever model or size grand you wanted. Taking it home with us and moving a few chairs and small tables, we realized we were in fact able to fit that 1927 masterpiece into one corner, with sufficient room for the bench.

Now all that remained was figuring out what to do with our existing Steinway and the upright at Kerrville. My busy brain went to work. Taking Maryann's problem into the equation, I thought we could have Monte take our Steinway console to Kerrville and bring back the upright and take it to Maryann. (We could figure out the payment deal later.) Then we could bring the Steinway grand in Fort Worth to our house as an early anniversary present. Voíla! It all worked like a charm—pianos were moved hither and yon, and everyone came out a winner. Even Byron, who loved hearing me play and practice, enjoyed our new grand piano, though he did say, "I never thought I'd be in the piano business!" That's just another indication of what a wonderful heart he had.

One time when Byron accompanied me to my weekly lesson in Lil's home, he noticed she needed a small table to sit between two chairs in her living room space. A week or so later, he brought her one, made in his shop from walnut hardwood. Lil was more thrilled than if I had suddenly sat down and played Beethoven's Ninth Symphony with no mistakes.

The final bit of piano business began during rehearsals for our Christmas musical at church. Amy and Andy Fambrough, the co-directors and members of our terrific praise team, had charged me with finding some sparkly necklaces for the ladies in the chorus to wear. When I brought some samples over to their home, I saw in the living area an old upright piano that was barely playable and needed a lot of work, Amy said. By the time we finished the musical, which was coincidentally about the time we sold our Kerrville home and brought the Steinway console back, I asked Andy during one rehearsal if he would like to have it. Oddly enough, he said yes. And they are still enjoying it today.

Andy recalls this fun story about Byron too:

One year we asked Byron to play Santa Claus in the Christmas program, and he accepted. Because he was having difficulty getting around, we put him in a high-backed chair, like a throne, attached casters to it, and used a ramp backstage so we could roll Byron in his chair onto the stage during the blackout. Then the dancers and singers would perform while he handed out presents to them just like Santa. What a hit he became! I know Byron had experienced a lot of big events in his life, but I think this was a first—he even made the local news channel on that one!

Now we were down to just one piano—the lovely 1927 Steinway Model M, and what a luxury it was. Every night before we went to bed, I'd sit and play for my great encourager, Byron, while he watched and smiled and listened and applauded. I even finally memorized his favorite piece, "Clair de Lune" by Claude Debussy. And I still play it every night. What dear, delightful memories! Try to tell me I'm not the most fortunate, blessed woman in the world—just try!

When I opened my office in Roanoke, I was totally amazed—and nervous—when Byron walked in, but he was so humble, kind, and gracious. When he learned I'd taken up golf, he'd always ask me about my game. I loved his smile and loved making him laugh. I guess the best way I could describe Byron is that he had a "clean soul." Though that might sound odd, that's how I always thought of him.

After I'd been playing golf for a while, Peggy and I were in a charity event, and all of a sudden here came Byron in a golf cart. Then I was *really* nervous! It just so happened that the next hole required a shot over water. Of course, I hit it thin, and it skipped a number of times before finally going under. Byron's comment? "I don't think I've ever seen a ball skip that many times before!" He was always encouraging to me, whether about golf, my work, or my family.

One year, Byron asked if I would come to the fitness trailer at his tournament so I could keep him loosened up for all he had to do. I did, and the other therapists didn't pay much attention to me at first, naturally. But when the call came in that Mr. Nelson was coming to the trailer to see me, their attitudes changed quite a bit. I remember pros like Fred Funk and Loren Roberts came in while he was there, and they just gathered around him like little kids, listening to his stories. He would brag about me to them so much it almost embarrassed me, but he would say, "I'm not just a-woofin'!"

Occasionally, when he'd come to the office, we'd get to talking about some pro athlete or celebrity who'd gotten in trouble some way. Byron's only comment was, "How can they expect God to bless them when they don't even go to church?"

A clean soul. That's what Byron had. A clean soul.

Daryl Laney, D.C.
Byron's chiropractor from 1989–2006

9

How to Play Golf with Your Spouse

Byron showed his sensitivity to my feelings and moods in many ways, and one of the most critical was golf. Having been a teacher for more than fifty years by then, he realized women need to be treated differently, and he was always gentle in his suggestions as we played together during the first year of our marriage. However I was something of a special case. I just knew I could figure out this simple game all by myself, thank you. While I certainly respected his experience, when we were on the course, I was forever thinking about my score and would brook very little distraction while I was endeavoring to make a seven instead of an eight or nine. Silly, wasn't it?

So, even though he made very few suggestions, within the first six months Byron saw there was a little problem. I would skull a chip across the green or chili-dip a pitch shot, and he would say, "Sweetheart, try that again with an eight iron this time."

I would reply (minus the sweetheart), "No!" Or I would try what he had recommended, and if it didn't work instantly, I would fling the offending club back into my bag and march on to the next hole without a word. I thought things were going swimmingly, but Lord Byron knew better.

One day in May 1987, I came home from Dallas where I was working on a writing assignment for Scottish Rite Hospital. Byron met me at the door with the latest issue of *Golf Digest* magazine in his hand.

"Sweetheart, I just read this article called 'How to Play Golf with Your Spouse,' and I want you to read it. I underlined everything I've been doing wrong, and I'm going to change, because if I don't change, you're not going to want to play golf with me anymore, and you may not even want to stay married to me!"

I melted, of course, as well as feeling like the world's biggest idiot. There I was, balking at advice from the greatest golfer/teacher ever, and he's taking all the blame for my frustration on the course. I took the magazine from his hands and sat down next to him. After a number of hugs and kisses and a few tears on my part, I read the article as he had instructed. Naturally the piece was not written for professional golfer husbands who had won five majors, fifty-four tournaments, eleven in a row, eighteen in a year, and taught other pros like Watson, Venturi, and Ward. No, it was designed more for the eighteen handicappers, who wouldn't know "you looked up" from U.S. Open rough.

We talked about it a little bit and finally figured out that, as silly as it was, I preferred to play on my own when I was on the course, instead of thinking all the time that he was going to want me to try another club or redo a shot. So from that moment on, he would only offer advice when I asked him during a round.

Oddly enough, that made it easier for me to ask, which I did a lot more often over the years. The result was that, even playing only once or twice a week, I went from a thirty to a sixteen. And let's not think about how much better I could have been if I had sat at the feet of this master of golf and tried to learn all I could about the game. As he told me years later, he really wouldn't have wanted me to get so gung-ho that I would be in single digits. He knew how much work that would take and felt it wouldn't have made me happy anyway. Byron always felt the happiest golfers he knew were the 80–85 shooters, who made enough pars to keep them happy, an occasional birdie for an extra lift, and the occasional double bogey to keep them humble.

Matching the Master

Oh, it was so much fun playing golf with him! Not only could Byron still play very well during the first several years of our marriage, but he seemed to get more enjoyment out of my occasional ripping good shot than he did his own. One time we were playing at Riverhill in Kerrville. I was a twenty-five handicap, and he was a ten. We were on the ninth tee, a great, really tough par four, and the forward tees were only a few yards ahead of the whites. He hit an excellent drive, and for once I tagged one that rolled a few yards past his ball.

After praising my drive, Byron hit a pure three-iron that ended up on the green about a foot away from the pin for a kick-in birdie. I, my brilliant drive notwithstanding, hit my three-wood amazingly fat and rolled the ball about thirty yards. Madder than a wet hen, I took out my four-iron, and thinking fairly murderous thoughts, swung blindly at that wretched thing. Blinking in amazement I watched it sail up and straight onto the green, where it disappeared into the hole for a three. And I got a stroke on the hole from Mr. Nelson that particular day.

You would think he'd be a little crestfallen after hitting two wonderful shots and getting an easy birdie but then getting beat by his floundering wife, thanks to that mysterious fiend known as "the rub of the green." No, my champion absolutely whooped with joy over it and proudly told the story dozens of times afterward to anyone who would listen. What a hero! "How to play golf with your spouse" indeed!

The Ace

With all our travels, we often took our clubs along and played when the opportunity arose. One place was in Naples, Florida, where we would visit dear friends Bud and Janet Waltz after being at the Players Championship. The course was Royal Poinciana, and we were playing with a couple of the Waltzes' friends. On about the fourth hole, a par three, there was a wooden sign on the tee box that listed the names and years of those who had made an ace there. I stared at it, thinking how amazing that must be to actually have your name on the tee box for everyone to see.

Then it was my turn to hit, so I took my five-iron for this 132-yard shot, made the smoothest swing of my life, and as the ball landed on the green, Byron called out, "It's going in!" And it did. I was stunned.

Unfortunately, I never hit a decent shot the rest of the round because I kept trying to figure out how to duplicate that one perfect swing.

Before we left the course, they had my name on that board, and the last I knew, it was still there—my one claim to golf fame.

My relationship with Byron was unique, as I became both his publicist and his friend, and it took me a couple of years to realize how extraordinary it was. It was not until 1992, at the unveiling of the bronze statue capturing his likeness, that I fully understood how revered he was in the local community and in the world of golf. It was during this time that I began being inundated with phone calls from sports writers around the world, who wanted to interview him around that time and during his eightieth year. It was through these requests, and hearing the reverence in the voices of the media, that I fully began to understand what he symbolized. I fielded hundreds of those media calls over the course of sixteen years, and I coordinated and sat in on many of the interviews. It was like watching a living history book.

As his friend and as a woman fifty years his junior, I can honestly say that no man in my life has ever treated me with as much respect and graciousness as Byron Nelson. He raised the bar for me in that regard. He wanted to make sure his friends felt loved. He wore his faith like a second skin, not like some heavy cloak. It made him happy, and he firmly believed "the Lord willing" that heaven would be his reward.

Angela Enright
Public Relations Director
Four Seasons Resort and Club

Media Mishaps

One of the remarkable things about playing golf with this amazing champion was that even though he was no longer competing, he still wanted to play his best, and he knew how to do it even when he couldn't execute the way he once did. But the only thing I or anyone else ever heard him say when he would hit a poor shot or—his version of golf's unforgivable sin, taking three from the edge—was, "You dog!" or "You dumb Dora."

That brings up a couple of interesting background stories. One involved a writer who did a book on the Masters champions through the 1980s. In the page on Byron the author quoted Byron as using a profanity, which he never did in all his life. When the book came out and Byron saw that, he called the writer and gently chided him, upon which the man looked back at his notes or reviewed the tape and later apologized. He said, "Byron, I'm so sorry, but I'm so accustomed to hearing so many other golfers swear that I just didn't realize your language was so different."

On another occasion an architect friend, with whom Byron had designed a number of courses, called to say a certain country club had written a history of their club, and Byron was quoted in it as using a truly disgusting obscenity. We later learned it was a story from an elderly member, who had evidently confused Byron with another player of his era. The books had already been printed, and we didn't want this to get into a big public mess, so Byron quietly went about letting the club know the truth of the matter. He supplied a story from that same tournament, which did happen to be both true and interesting, and strongly encouraged them to excise the offending page and tip in a new one with the correction. Fortunately they did, and we haven't heard any more about it. But it was a good lesson on the need to be careful about how things are printed regarding someone who is in the public eye. Even though it was widely known that toward the end of Ben Hogan's career he had a dreadful problem with putting, some writer here or there would get Ben confused with Byron and write that Byron had the yips, which he never did. But once something gets into print, it develops a life of its own, and it's difficult to erase.

In Byron's case he would occasionally say, "I'm not concerned with what they write about me, as long as it's factual." He was also aware that as hard as he had worked all his life to earn a good reputation, he didn't want that to be tarnished by someone not doing their homework and printing an untruth that might negatively affect him in some way or disillusion youngsters who were looking to imitate him in golf or in life.

Mike Massad Sr., who is a member of the Salesmanship Club and was 1978 chairman of the Byron Nelson Golf Classic Tournament, says, "Byron always had time for others. He was an accomplished listener and took the time to hear you. If it was something about your golf game, he would first listen intently, then give you an idea. I never heard Byron speak a single vulgar word. He always took the time to ask God to guide, guard, and direct him, and he followed the Lord's advice." And I think that about sums it up.

Tournaments and Tricks

As I grew in wisdom and power and chipping and putting under his tutelage, I did begin to play in club tournaments. One year I was in the finals for the first flight of the club championship. I was playing on the Four Seasons' Tournament Players Club (TPC) Course, and it was quite a contest. My opponent was one of these wonder women who could hit a three-iron 210 yards, so I figured I had no chance. But I calmed my nerves on the first tee by telling myself that I couldn't do any worse than second, and off we went. Amazingly the match was over on sixteen, and I was actually the winner, no doubt because I was so relaxed I just played my own game and let her make a few more mistakes than I did. But we were friends and decided to go ahead and play the last two holes for fun. As we stepped on to the eighteenth tee, a tricky little thought came into my head.

I saw up near the green a small gallery waiting for us. I could also see The Hat gleaming among them all. So I decided to let my opponent tee off first, knowing Byron would think the match was still on and she had won the seventeenth. As we finished on eighteen, I shook her hand and waved to my sweetheart, so he knew I had actually won. He didn't know whether to be mad or glad for me. But even if it was a little wicked, I figured it was good for him. And of course, he forgave me for it . . . almost right away.

Through all those twenty years, in fact, there was only one time Byron became upset with me. I had laboriously moved a marble-topped chest in our bedroom. It was a foolish thing to do, I suppose, but I ingeniously figured out how to move the marble top off the chest and onto the bed, then move the much lighter chest where I wanted it, and slide the marble top back on.

At that moment, I heard an ominous, "Now, honey!" from the doorway and turned to see him standing there with his hands on his hips and the first frown I had seen. He hadn't yet realized that I was a determined little scamp, who didn't like to ask for help with such things. Admittedly, it would have made more sense and been much less work to have done it together. He was concerned that, if it hadn't gone as I had planned, I could have been badly hurt if that marble had dropped on my foot or something. And he was right. So I never moved that chest again . . . at least, not when he was around.

Byron set the tone for so many relationships by being the first to reach out, disarming his celebrity status. I was fortunate to get to spend almost ten years as his friend. To me, Byron's most unusual characteristic was peace—his whole manner simply exuded peace. He was still when those around him were hurried. He was calm when he was at the center of attention. He was deliberate when it mattered most to people. He was confident when people needed hope the most. And the most important thing I learned from him was consistency. Not surprisingly, this was the hallmark of his golf career, one that I only got to read about. Byron's consistency in his faith, his thoughts, his manner with people, and even his physical stature was remarkable. Byron's goal was to be a Christian gentleman. He succeeded at that more than anyone else I have ever known.

Paul Earnest
Director of Golf,
Four Seasons Resort and Club

10

An Unforgettable Secretary's Day

Another important stop on Byron's list of people for me to meet was the Salesmanship Club of Dallas, which had been sponsoring and running the tournament with Byron's name on it since 1968. His first opportunity to do that was on Secretary's Day the following April. There I was, sitting with Byron on the dais at the Dallas Country Club, looking out at a sea of hundreds of members of the Salesmanship Club accompanied by their top office assistants. By this time I was already helping Byron with his voluminous correspondence, typing and mailing and filing letters and autograph requests, and that had been quite an education for me.

After the invocation was given and announcements were made, Byron got up to speak, and here's what he said:

"It certainly is great to see all you fellows here today, and it's especially great to see your secretaries. I know you ladies are a great help to your bosses, especially as they get ready to go to work on the tournament. Peggy has already been helping me a lot with my correspondence and such. But you men, I've got to tell you, I've got a better deal than any of you"—here Byron paused for just a split second—then added, "because I get to sleep with my secretary!"

No one in that room ever expected to hear Byron Nelson say anything like that, and the whole place exploded with laughter and applause, while my face, as our friend Steve Barley told me later, blushed red as a fire truck. I laughed along with Byron, because it was plain to see everyone was happy for him, so I couldn't possibly fuss about it.

See what I mean about the surprising Mr. Nelson?

I See You Just Cost Me $25,000

I did know Byron well enough in other areas, and one example occurred about six months after we were married. One morning, after Byron had gone out to the woodshop, the phone rang. I answered it and a young man from some marketing company asked for Byron. In my best secretarial voice, I told him Mr. Nelson was busy and asked if I could help. It turned out his company had the maker of a well-known brand of scotch whiskey for a client and wanted to use Byron's picture in an ad. I was familiar with the campaign, similar to the Rolex pieces where they write about athletes' accomplishments and compare their achievements to the product's excellent qualities. I knew without a doubt that Byron would have no interest in promoting whiskey and politely told him so.

"But we would pay him $25,000," the young fellow said.

I responded, "You're welcome to send him a letter about it if you wish, but I'm quite certain he'll say no."

We both hung up, and a few minutes later I walked out to the shop to see how Byron was getting along with his project. As it happened he was outside, sanding a large piece of wood so the breeze would blow the dust away. He looked up as I approached and said with a twinkle in his eyes, "I see you just cost me $25,000!" It seemed that Mr. Nelson had picked up the phone in the shop at the same time I did in the house and heard the entire conversation but didn't say a word. At first I didn't know if he was kidding, but then I saw that twinkle and knew I had done the right thing, thankfully.

Byron had already told me—during that "list of sixteen things" conference we'd had earlier—that we would be living on his income from the investments he and Louise had made over the years. When we were married he had only one small outside contract, so while we weren't exactly pinching pennies, and Byron was extraordinarily generous with me, we did nothing extra in the way of decorating or travel those first few years. So that conversation with the marketing fellow could have had me on just slightly shaky ground!

Clubs, Clothes, and Courses

Byron and I have been very blessed by our CPA and business manager, Jon Bradley of the Weaver and Tidwell firm in Dallas, who took expert charge of all Byron's contracts and endorsements, beginning with Roger Cleveland. It was about 1988 when Byron decided he'd like to have some new persimmon woods, and he knew Roger Cleveland of Cleveland Golf in California made some pretty terrific wedges that a lot of the boys on the tour were using. So he called Roger and asked him for a driver.

Roger sent a beautiful persimmon-headed driver, but unfortunately, the heat it likely encountered during shipping had caused the stockinet cover on the head to stick and dulled the finish. So Byron called Roger and gently broke the news. As it happened it was just a couple of weeks before the Masters, and Byron had been asked to be one of the honorary starters along with Gene Sarazen and Sam Snead. He was really hoping to have a new driver to use that day. When we arrived in Augusta on Tuesday morning and headed toward the clubhouse, there was Roger in person, and in his hands was a brand-new, shiny-headed, perfectly finished persimmon driver, which Byron used that Thursday morning and for several years afterward.

In fact, Byron was so impressed with Roger's response he then asked him to create a set of irons with Byron's name on them, like the ones he'd had years before when he was connected with MacGregor Golf Company in Dayton. Roger took that suggestion on the run, and soon there was a whole set of beautiful irons that proved to be a great success for Roger's company, as well as providing Byron with some excellent clubs with which to play.

Later Jon Bradley was instrumental in helping start a golf clothing line with Byron's name on it. Jimmy Haggar of the Haggar apparel family was the design genius who created a series of handsome and distinctive shirts, sweaters, and slacks that were both comfortable for golf and classy enough to make the transition from the office to the course and back. Though the clothing line has changed hands several times, now with Legends Golf, Byron was so delighted to have his name on fine quality clothing that worked for golf and everything else short of black-tie affairs.

Through the years Byron also had opportunities to work on a number of golf course design projects with several excellent architects. His two favorites were Jay Morrish and Joe Finger. Both of these men were excellent architects with a deep love for the game, but two more different personalities one could scarcely hope to find on the same planet. Yet Byron was somehow able to blend his ideas and experience as both player and teacher with their earth-moving expertise and engineering knowledge. Together both Joe and Byron and Jay and Byron produced some remarkable and playable, yet challenging courses.

One of Byron's last two golf course design projects was in Japan, which was just astonishing for him. If you go to Iwaki City, 120 miles north of Tokyo today, you might get to play at the Byron Nelson Country Club, which Byron designed with golf professional D. A. Weibring in 1991. And last, but perhaps the most unusual, is Headwaters Club at Teton Springs in Victor, Idaho, just across the border from Jackson Hole, Wyoming, which combines golf and fly-fishing at the same location, right at the foot of the beautiful Grand Teton Mountains.

I was fortunate enough to become Byron's accountant in the spring of 1978. Our relationship expanded in the late 1980s to include reviewing all his endorsement opportunities and ultimately becoming his confidant. The more you're around Byron, the more you appreciate him. He was my best friend.

The most unusual quality I saw in Byron was his ability to focus on others and not himself, even with all his accomplishments and fame. This quality made him the most humble man I've ever known. One day, before the autographing craze got out of hand, I was at Byron's home, sitting in his office talking about some business matter. I asked Byron to find a document I needed from him and he began looking through the stack of papers on his desk.

Suddenly he held up a letter and said, "Oh my!" I asked what was wrong and Byron said, "This fan letter got lost in my papers, and it's been here over two months!" Then I watched in total amazement as Byron dialed information, got the man's phone number, and called him to apologize for responding so slowly. Ask yourself what famous person would you expect to do that. Byron is the only one who comes to my mind. He taught me that life is about giving and not taking. Of course, he was right. My best remembrances are about the warm feelings we get from helping others.

Jon Bradley
CPA and Business Manager

11

The Only One Who
Never Disappointed Me

One of the sixteen things on that list Byron had for me was the prospect of his upcoming hernia surgery, which was already scheduled for December 9, just a few weeks after our wedding. When he was in recovery, the doctors let me see him, and he looked up at me groggily and said, "You're so pretty . . . you're so pretty!" Can you imagine? I was thrilled, of course, and amazed.

His recovery went very well; in fact, the next week we went back to Kerrville, and since he couldn't play golf yet, we busied ourselves rearranging furniture and rehanging paintings and such. Once again Byron displayed remarkable patience and charm, holding up each piece of original art that he and Louise had carefully collected over the years while I would say profound things like, "About an inch higher, sweetheart," or "Half an inch to the left." When we were finished (meaning when I got fatigued from all the decisions), we were both pretty satisfied. Apparently he really meant that I would be queen of the house, only now there were two!

We began to take regular trips to our Kerrville retreat as the weather improved, but we figured out quickly that because Byron was in such demand, we would need to make these vacations a regularly scheduled thing, or we would never get to go. We settled on the first week of the month, leaving the ranch on Monday and coming back Friday.

The next month we were packing up to take off that first Monday when the phone rang. Byron answered it, talked a little while, hung up and said, "We can't go, sweetheart. Somebody from the press wants to make some pictures with me."

I looked at him and said, "Well, let's just sell the place then." He just looked at me for a long minute. Then without a word he picked up the phone, called whoever it was back, and rescheduled the photo session for the following week. That's how we did it. Byron was such a humble hero it hardly ever occurred to him that he had at least as much say-so in these things as the person on the other end.

Byron's nephew, Bryan Mitchell, talked about Byron's humility too, saying,

Byron was constant. He was the same person no matter what group of people he might be placed in. That was true whether it was politicians, sports figures, or celebrities, versus those with lesser means or no recognition among peers. Many people would call those "common folks," but not Byron. He valued every person he encountered and wanted the best for each. He was truly Jesus to every person he met. All of that can be summed up in one word: *humility*. Byron was a humble man, whom so many held in high esteem and awe, but he genuinely never understood what the big fuss was about!

Writing and Ghostwriting

One of the many delights in being married to Byron was getting to know his friends. Not too long after the wedding, we were invited to dinner at Dallas Country Club with several other couples, and I was seated next to Felix McKnight, a longtime sportswriter and editor for the Dallas paper. At one point during the meal, Felix confided in me that throughout his career he had met and interviewed all of the greats in every sport. And with a kind of awed look in his eyes, he said, "Byron is the only one who never disappointed me." Quite an encomium from someone in the sports celebrity business, I thought. After twenty years with Byron, I completely agree.

Another longtime friend was Jim Chambers, publisher of the *Dallas Times Herald* and the one who helped Byron start his career in sports commentating by ghostwriting his columns about the tournament. We went to dinner at Jim and Betty's home one evening, and Jim gently chaffed me by asking if I had played Preston Trail yet. Fortunately Byron had filled me in that Preston Trail was a men-only club, so I looked at Mr. Chambers and said, "Not yet, but I'm really looking forward to it," with a smile that told him I knew he was teasing me, and everyone got a good laugh out of it.

Shortly after that, Jim learned I had some experience as a writer. Since the hospital he was connected with, Texas Scottish Rite Hospital for

Children, needed a written history, he gave me the assignment. It proved interesting, because the hospital treated every patient for free and had an excellent record for advancements in treating scoliosis, dyslexia, and other childhood disorders. Writing the book gave me a great opportunity to learn more about the history of Dallas's early leaders, many of whom were also involved in the Salesmanship Club.

Our First Masters, April 1987

As if being married to Mr. Wonderful weren't enough, our first golf tournament trip was to the cathedral of golf, Augusta National Golf Club in Georgia for the 1987 Masters. I was a little shy about meeting all these golf greats from around the world, but I was so excited to be there with Byron I wasn't concerned so much about passing anybody else's test. Byron warned me gently that as he was playing a few practice holes with Tom Watson or in the Par 3 Contest, I might hear some things from folks in the gallery that I wouldn't necessarily like. He was right, but not in quite the way he had thought.

The first day after we arrived, he and Tom were playing the back nine together, and both were on the twelfth green at fabled Amen Corner. Suddenly I overheard someone in a group in front of me say, "Who's that playing with Watson?"

Another replied, "That's Byron Nelson. I heard he married some woman twenty years younger than he is!" I nearly laughed out loud and toyed with the idea of nudging the fellow and saying, "No, it's worse than that!" But not wanting to draw any attention to myself, I decided against it.

Later, as Tom and Byron were toiling up the eighteenth fairway—a much steeper hill than it appears on television—two young men near me were also spectating, and one said, "Who's that with Watson?"

I helpfully offered, "I think that's Byron Nelson," to which they both nodded in recognition, and then one said, "That's pretty rough, making that old guy walk up that hill!" Judging from the shape these guys were in, they might have had a little trouble with it themselves.

The next day at the Par 3 course, after Tom and Byron teed off, I was walking along next to two pretty young things in their mid-twenties, and one said of Byron, "I wonder how old he is?"

The other said, "I wonder how rich he is!"

I just managed to overcome the urge to tap her on the shoulder and say, "He's not rich enough for you, honey." Aren't you proud of me?

Then came Thursday morning and the opening of the actual tournament, led off in grand style by Byron, Gene Sarazen, and Sam Snead as honorary starters. They would play nine holes together, and

I loved Byron as a friend, teacher, and confidant. The most unusual quality I saw in Byron was his sense of humor and fun. He really liked to ham it up on the golf course. What I learned from him was how to speak in front of people. His honesty and humility were the canvas from which he spoke. To me Byron epitomized what is right with the human race.

Tom Watson
Professional Golfer and Dear Friend

there were thousands of people following these great legends of the game. Byron had a great time that day, chipping in for a birdie on the sixth hole, and then pitching in for a tremendous par on the ninth. He told me later he was just trying to impress me. He succeeded.

I remember meeting the wonderful amateur Bill Campbell, a gentleman of great renown, on the first tee. About the second or third hole, I also got to meet Don Spencer, a super young man who worked for the United States Golf Association (USGA) at the time. Both men were great admirers of the game, but they clearly had a regard for Byron that was different from their other friendships. I was to learn over and over through the years that everyone who ever met him for even a few minutes would see something in him that was above and beyond ordinary—not just for his golf, but for something about his character. Byron himself never understood it, though he was often made aware of it, and downplayed it as much as possible.

He would say, "I'm not famous—just a lot of people know me is all." He was genuinely puzzled by people's admiration, saying, "I don't know why people think so much of me—I'm not doing anything any different from what anybody ought to do."

That's the trouble, Mr. Nelson. Most of us aren't doing what we ought to do enough of the time.

Byron's words would make a pretty good epitaph, wouldn't they?

Learning about "Magnolia"

Among the great treats of that first Masters trip was meeting and getting to stay with Byron's dear friends Phil and Gracie Harison. In the early years Byron and Louise had often stayed with Phil's parents, and later with Phil and Gracie. This remarkable couple was kind enough to include me. Phil Jr. met us at the airport, and I mistakenly took him to be no more than eighteen. The truth was he had already graduated from college and was working in his father's insurance business. He drove us to his parents' beautiful home, and as we entered the house, Gracie

I can be a better person." I think for me that sums up the overall effect Byron had on me. One of the most interesting stories that struck me was about the time Byron traveled to the West Coast from Texas. His biggest concern wasn't the events themselves or his competitors; it was how many spare tires it would take to make the trip and get back home.

Another highlight for me was sitting at dinner with my wife Chris, Peggy, Tom Lehman, Jim Furyk, and of course Lord Byron. This was the week following the EDS Byron Nelson Championship in 2005. Tom Lehman was the 2005 Captain of the Ryder Cup, and to hear the stories of Byron's Ryder Cup experiences was amazing. For me, sitting at the same table with three of the greatest golfers of all time was priceless.

Following the dinner we all took a walking tour of Fairway Ranch with Byron leading in his personalized golf cart—a walk I will never forget, ending with the sun setting as I watched Chris and Byron walk back to the house. It was a very emotional moment that topped off an incredible evening. That was the last time I had with Byron. The picture with the sunset is certainly more meaningful to me today.

I know now why my dad, Milt Lindstrom, named me after Byron Nelson.

Byron Dana Lindstrom
Vice President of Sales, Finis, Inc.
Byron's Namesake and Our Friend since 1996

came fluttering down the hallway toward us, saying, "Isn't the pollen awful this year?" To my Yankee ears, though, her "pollen" sounded like "pielin," so I looked to Byron for help. But he couldn't figure it out either, and after I said excuse me a few more times, Gracie explained, "The pielin—that awful yellow stuff that comes down off the trees and gets all over your shoes and your car."

So began my introduction to the Deep South. I find that accent to be very soothing and enchanting much of the time, but on occasion, it can create some downright bewilderment for me. In fact, although nearly everyone I met on that first trip had some of that lilt to their speech, I was told that Gracie alone had the ultimate version, known to the cognoscenti as "magnolia." And we all loved her for it.

Phil, Gracie's equally charming husband, had carried on his father's tradition as official starter for the tournament. It was always a treat to hear him announcing the players' names with no extra folderol or publicity. He simply said, "Mr. Nick Price now driving—fore, please."

Everything at the Masters was always so stately and dignified without being in the least stuffy. What a privilege it was to be there at all, but even more so to be with Byron. Indeed they would invite both of us to sit on the first tee and enjoy watching the players teeing off right in front of us. That was fun, though I know that for some of them finding Mr. Nelson there when they were already nervous as a cat on hot bricks wasn't exactly helping their equilibrium any.

Every year after that we got to enjoy the same lovely times, usually leaving on Monday and coming home on Friday, watching the last two rounds in the comfort of our own home. But one year I asked if we couldn't stay for the whole tournament, sit down there at Amen Corner and watch the players come through. That happened to be the year it rained steadily the whole weekend, so on Sunday we sat in the clubhouse with a bunch of other wet folks and watched the play on television until it was time to leave for the airport. We heard in the air between Augusta and Atlanta that Nick Faldo had beaten Raymond Floyd in a playoff, and that sealed it. We never stayed for the whole tournament again.

Fortunately for us, when Jack Stephens became chairman, he also had great regard for Byron. He had learned about the difficulty we had navigating the flight changes in Atlanta, due to Byron's recent hip surgeries and needing a cane to get around. Jack insisted on flying us to and from the Masters in one of his own planes. It didn't take us long to agree, and from then on, we felt as if we were living in the tallest cotton anywhere. Jack was so shy that he would hardly let us even say thank you; it was such a pleasure for him to do something for Byron, because Byron had been so good to the game and to the Masters tournament.

Byron, Gene, and Sam continued as honorary starters, but within a couple of years, it simply wasn't possible for them to play nine holes, so they would just hit an honorary tee shot. Soon Byron began to be a little uncomfortable with that, since he really wasn't playing much anymore, and after Gene died, Byron just decided to politely decline. He had served on the tournament improvements committee for years and felt he could contribute a lot more that way than hitting a short slice or decking someone in the gallery as Snead had done one year, and I was totally on his side. It was a difficult thing for him to say no to Mr. Stephens, because we were both so grateful for his help with the travel, but Jack was very understanding and still insisted on flying us to Augusta as long as we were able to come.

12

The Pro and the Pros

With all our travels to the majors and other tournaments, plus special events connected with golf, I naturally met a number of the big golf names (though prejudiced as I am, I never felt any of them were bigger than Byron). We would go to the Players Championship, the U.S. Open sometimes, the PGA championship, and a few others, such as the Colonial. It was always fun to be there with Byron and see the respect and affection everyone felt for him, especially the pros.

One year we were invited to the Champions' Dinner prior to the start of the Players Championship in Ponte Vedra, Florida. By that time I had known Byron long enough and well enough to be intrigued by the fact that every time he dreamed about golf, it was filled with anxiety. In his dreams he had lost his clubs, couldn't find the first tee, or something equally dreadful. So as we were sitting across from Jack Nicklaus and Tom Kite at the dinner, I decided to ask those two stars if they ever dreamed about golf as Byron did and what those dreams were like.

"Terrible!" said Tom immediately. "I can never find my five-iron!"

Jack chimed in with, "Awful—just awful." His golf dreams were apparently so bad he didn't even want to talk about them.

I found that fascinating, because it seemed to say a lot about the drive and the pressure they felt to always win at this demanding game of imperfection.

I had met Hale Irwin first, at that unforgettable reunion with Mr. Nelson after five years, but being a tournament volunteer and sticking very close to Byron whenever we traveled, I got to know many of the players fairly well, at least by sight. Through the years as the prize money began to explode, the top players were rolling in greenbacks a lot more comfortably than Byron's generation ever thought of doing.

The first year they began the Payne Stewart Award, Byron and I were seated on the stage at the opening ceremony. I was next to Billy Andrade, one of the thirty players in the Tour Championship played at Eastlake in Atlanta, Bob Jones's home course. That was the first year the top thirty pros had each won more than a million dollars on tour. Billy asked me how I was, and I said, "I'm really excited—I've never been on a stage with thirty millionaires before!"

One of the greatest things about golf, though, is that virtually all of these professionals are wonderful fellows, very down-to-earth, and well aware of their good fortune. They realize that much of the credit for their success is owed to the pioneers like Hagen,

Byron at NCR Country Club for Bogey Busters event in 1981—the year we met.

Playing golf at the Four Seasons in Irving, Texas, shortly before our marriage in 1986.

Peggy, Lucy McDonald (my mom), and Byron—wedding day, November 15, 1986.

Byron with our sons, Stanton (top) and John (right) Tangeman on the 18th tee at Riverhill Country Club, Kerrville, Texas.

My favorite dishwasher in the kitchen at Fairway Ranch.

Peggy and Byron in front of Robert Summers' 9'6" bronze statue of Byron near the first tee of Four Seasons TPC. Presented on Byron's 80th birthday, February 4, 1992.

Byron with our cherry bookcase—his woodworking pride and joy. This photo appeared in Wood magazine in March 1992.

Tom Watson and Byron before the Champions Dinner at Augusta National Golf Club, c1994. Photo by Frank Christian.

Peggy, Byron and Peggy's horse, Peppy Lee Bueno

Bob Hope, Tanya Tucker, and Byron in San Antonio, Texas.

Peggy, Erin Baggs, Maeci Baggs, and Byron with horses at North Texas State Fair for 4H competition.

Former President George H.W. Bush, Peggy, Byron, and Barbara Bush at Tres Amigos benefit gala in Houston, Texas, 1997.

Tim Finchem, Peggy, Arnold Palmer, and Byron at PGA Tour Awards Banquet at LaJolla, California, late 1990s.

Byron (age 87) and his first grandson, Finn Henry Tangeman, 1999.

Byron and Peggy with bronze caddie statue, a gift from Peggy for Byron's birthday, 2000.

Byron and Peggy at the Christmas party (c2002) for the Women's Golf Association, members of The Sports Club at the Four Seasons Resort.

Peggy and Byron at Oilmen's Golf Tournament in Jasper Park Lodge, Canada, on "Song of the South" costume night.

Byron on redwood swing he made for the porch at Fairway Ranch.

Byron and Peggy at Par 3 Contest during the 2003 Masters at Augusta.

Cherée Johnson, Marcia Baggs—Peggy's best friends—and Peggy in the living room at Fairway Ranch, 2003. They are better known as the "Aha Sisters."

Peggy and Byron at the opening ceremonies for his tournament, 2004.

Byron congratulating Sergio Garcia for winning the EDS Byron Nelson Championship, May 2004.

Maria and Nadia Richardson, Russian girls adopted by our friends Matt and M. J. Richardson.

(Back row) Peggy and Byron (Front Row) Eddie, Maeci, Erin, and Marcia Baggs in the living room at Fairway Ranch.

Randy Travis holding three wooden crosses Byron made for him, commemorating Randy's song, "Three Wooden Crosses"—a 2003 Dove Award winner—Randy's wife, Lib, Byron, and Peggy

Peggy and Byron at Bear Creek Golf Course in Fort Worth, 2005, for fundraiser.

Judy Stead and Peggy, best friends since college days in 1962.

Byron Nelson High School, Trophy Club, Texas, dedicated October 18, 2009.

Peggy accepting Byron's Congressional Gold Medal for Humanitarian Service announced a few weeks before he died but presented posthumously in Washington, D. C., June 2007.

Byron watching players on the 18th green at his tournament on Sunday afternoon.

Sarazen, Hogan, and Nelson, and the example of gentlemanliness and good sportsmanship so many of the early pros displayed.

> I knew Byron for sixty years, and they were all good. He was a great friend, the same person all the time, very enjoyable to be with, easy to talk to. Byron was remarkable as a great example to young golfers trying to make a living at the game. He was amazingly consistent as a player, and that was the thing he took the most pride and pleasure in about his game, more than any victory or major, and he was consistent as a great person too.
>
> *Ross T. Collins*
> *Golf Professional and National Left-Handed Golf Champion*

Byron really enjoyed his twin careers, first as a pro and then as a broadcaster, and we watched a lot of golf together either in person or on television. But because his own game was so consistent, he found it difficult to understand how a player could win a tournament one week and miss the cut the next, even though he knew there was a lot more money on the tour than in his heyday when you had to be in the top ten just to have enough money to get to the next tournament down the road. He did understand and admire the determination the pros have today to pay more attention to their families and business interests and not to need to be on the road thirty or more weeks out of the year. But he surely did want us to get that Ryder Cup back!

However the last six months of his life on earth, Byron pretty much lost interest in watching golf at all. Several of his favorite players were struggling with their games, at least from what we could see on the air, and as much as Byron would have liked to help them, he didn't presume to interfere with the coaches they had already. He rarely criticized anyone's game out loud. About the only thing he would say was, "Well, he's become a pretty good par shooter." For the guys on the tour, that would have amounted to a criticism of the worst sort.

Byron had to stop playing when he was ninety; he simply didn't have the strength to stand and swing and feel stable on his feet. The last time he played was at Riverhill in Kerrville. I know it bothered him to give it up, but he didn't say much about it. I gave up playing myself about the same time, because it was a lot more fun to be at home with him than making triple bogeys somewhere.

Still Byron had tremendous admiration for the exceptional behavior of nearly everyone he knew in golf. There were few departures from that standard, and those stood out as lessons in how *not* to live one's life. Even when he was disappointed in someone's behavior, particularly people in the public eye, whether athletes, politicians, or celebrities in other arenas, he would only say, "You just can't expect much from people who don't know the Lord."

Travel, Travel, and More Travel!

For someone who had never cared about seeing the world outside of Ohio, life with Byron was quite a change in the travel department. Over the years we went to Augusta sixteen times, to Canada at least six times, to Japan three times, to Scotland, Ireland, San Francisco, San Diego, Los Angeles, Florida, Chicago, Colorado, Seattle, Louisville, New York, North Carolina, Pennsylvania, Kansas City, Oklahoma, Montana, Wyoming, Arizona, New Mexico, New Jersey, New Orleans,

St. Louis, Las Vegas, Indiana, Michigan, Oregon, Boston, Vermont, New Hampshire, Connecticut, Washington D.C., and Prince Edward Island. Whew! It wears me out just thinking about it.

While traveling was never my ambition, I did enjoy flying, and of course, being with Byron made everything worthwhile. He was a delightful travel companion. He always took care of the luggage, tickets, hotels, and tips, continually making me feel like the "Queen of All Queens," one of his favorite pet names for me.

We collected lots of pleasant memories and formed new friendships on many of these trips, but the ones that stand out the most in my mind were two trips to Washington, D.C. The first was in 1992, celebrating Byron's and Sam Snead's eightieth birthdays and Gene Sarazen's ninetieth by visiting President George H. W. Bush in the Oval Office. One of the crazy things about that day was that in my naiveté I didn't take any form of identification with me, and when the security fellow asked me for mine, I just pointed to Byron and said, "I'm with him." Apparently the guy didn't think anyone so clueless could be a threat, so I passed.

After the photo shoot in the Oval Office, President Bush ushered Byron, Sam Snead, Gene Sarazen, and me out to his putting clock, handed each of us a putter, and invited us to hit a few. So there I was in my flowered silk dress and high heels and no glasses, fairly frozen in time. But I stepped over to the ball, swatted it at a hole about eight feet away, and wonder of wonders, it went in. I handed the putter back, said, "Thank you, Mr. President," and I was finished.

The next trip to D.C., in June 2007, was without Byron when I accepted his Congressional Gold Medal for Humanitarian Service.

The day after the ceremony in the Capitol, we visited President George W. Bush in the Oval Office, and when I showed him Byron's medal, he asked, "Is this really gold?" All I could think of to say was, "Well sir, that's what they told me."

On a more personal note, perhaps our two other favorite trips were to Seattle and Los Angeles for John's and Stan's weddings to Anne and Hope, respectively. They were such special days, and we have been so blessed with those two delightful young women, who have been wonderful mates to our sons, as well as terrific mothers to our five grandsons—Finn, Floyd, Reed, Oliver, and Charlie.

I was fortunate to win the 2005 EDS Byron Nelson Championship, and because of that one victory I was able to spend some time with Byron at the J. Erik Jonsson Community School in Dallas supported by the Salesmanship Club through Byron's tournament. Byron loved golf and supported those of us who are professional golfers. He would write a letter each week to whichever pro had won a tournament, and it became an added bonus for each of those winners. Tiger Woods has saved all of his letters from Byron, and mine are in frames for all to see.

Byron took the time one year to go to the nursery at the Four Seasons and have his picture taken with all of the pros' children, and his love for children and willingness to take the time to do that has inspired me to do the same. My wife and I support the Stepping Stone Foundation in Phoenix because of Byron's influence.

Ted Purdy
Professional Golfer and
2005 EDS Byron Nelson Tournament Champion

The HP Byron Nelson Championship

After coming home from Augusta, it was time to gear up for the Byron Nelson tournament. I had no idea how much hard work and organization it took to put on this amazing golf event—and I barely understand it yet today. But I knew I wanted to be involved at least on the fringes, so I threw my volunteer hat in the ring and began doing a small portion of the hard work the ladies did. I did ten years as a walking scorer, one stint in the nursery, another dozen years on transportation, several as a greenside scorer, worked in the media room back when we physically put the scores on the big board, and did a couple of turns as a hostess at the information booth near the first tee.

The last year I worked on transportation I was assigned to go to the airport to pick up Retief Goosen, the great U.S. Open champion from South Africa, who was playing in our tournament for the first time. I asked Byron if he would like to go with me, since he was by himself at tournament headquarters and was finished with his autographing and interviews for the morning. He quickly agreed and off we went to Dallas's Love Field, where I met Mr. Goosen as he was coming into the terminal. After introducing myself I told him I had someone in the car who really wanted to meet him, and the look on his face was quite a study, since he had no idea who it might be. When he saw Byron, though, he was pleased, surprised, and relieved. Oddly enough, all the way back to the course they talked about farming and cattle, because Retief's parents had a farm in South Africa, so they had many things in common. When Retief went into the press room that afternoon, he talked about how special it was that Byron came to meet him at the airport, never knowing it was just one of those little miracles we get to enjoy on this earth.

The real kicker, though, was that because Byron was alone at headquarters when I invited him to come along, we never thought to leave a note about where we were going. When his driver, our dear friend Steve Barley, came back from lunch and Byron was MIA, he had a conniption fit. I was in rather deep trouble with Steve that day.

My favorite job proved to be helping to pack the hundreds of volunteer lunches that had to be transported out to the marshals, spotters, and greenside scorers all around both courses. It was always the fastest forty-five minutes of my life as we shoved sandwiches, chips, cookies, mustard, mayonnaise, and napkins into bags and packed them into cardboard boxes for the vans to rush them out to those hungry folks who couldn't leave their posts. It was great fun, lots of laughs, and I've been pretty lucky—so far, I haven't been rained on one time, but I'm sure that record will be broken one of these years.

The tournament bearing his name was very important to Byron. And Steve Barley, Byron's friend and confidant since 1978, recalls why:

> When I was tournament chairman, one of my greatest satisfactions was using Byron's quote as part of our tournament art, because it captured his feeling about having the event named for him: "It's the greatest thing that's ever happened to me in golf—better than winning the Masters or the U.S. Open or the eleven in a row, because it helps people."

That was my Byron.

13

Isn't He a Rascal?

Perhaps one of the strangest things about our marriage was that I could hardly think of Byron as old, or even much older than I was. Maybe that was partly because we both liked so many of the same things, including old movies. We only went to one movie at a theater in twenty years, and that one was *The Passion of the Christ*. It took Jesus to get us there! Today's movies certainly aren't what they were in the 1930s and '40s, and so much of what's out there is pure poison, in my opinion.

I never thought much about the difference in our ages, even according to appearance. Other folks did, though, and occasionally it would cause a little embarrassment. Someone would see us at a tournament, come up to me and ask, "Are you Byron's daughter?" When I would smilingly reply that I was actually his wife, they would be covered with blushes and apologize all over the place, which made me feel awful, because it was a pretty natural mistake to make.

So I had a brilliant idea one day, and the next person who asked that same question got this answer instead: "No, I'm his wife. Isn't he a rascal?" And they would look surprised and then say, "Yes, he is!" and we would both get a chuckle out of it. Early on, at Jack Nicklaus's Memorial tournament one year, a young fellow actually asked if I was Byron's granddaughter, but I figured he just needed better glasses.

Speaking of appearances, Byron never thought he was good looking, just very ordinary—"a plain old Joe," as he would say. And in some photos he does look pretty average. But there are many pictures of him looking drop-dead gorgeous, and we often had conversations that went like this:

Me: "You're so handsome!"

Byron: "Well, nobody ever told me that till you came along."

Once in a while, I'd ask, "Didn't Louise think you were handsome?"

He would say, "Oh, she thought I looked all right, but she never said much about it."

I knew that when Byron met Louise back in Texarkana, she had been seeing a young man who worked at the bank. Byron moved that young fellow out of the picture rapidly, and he was never heard from again.

So one time we were having the same conversation on the way to church one Wednesday evening, and when he said, "Oh, she thought I looked okay, but no one ever said I was handsome but you."

I asked, "Were you better looking than that bank clerk?"

Instant, emphatic reply: "Yes, I was!"

He was a humble man for sure, but he was also refreshingly honest.

Memories that Keep Me Smiling

Just about anyone who ever spent time talking with Byron marveled at how good his memory was. It seemed as if he could recall every shot in every tournament and sometimes a lot of the shots the other guys were making too. He did have a remarkable memory for lots of things and for people, though he met so many hundreds of folks he couldn't always call their names. When he had forgotten, he would always ask them again, which I thought was a sweet thing for him to do. The man whose memory he really admired was the great sportscaster Chris Schenkel, who truly was phenomenal. He had trained himself in that area from the time he first began calling the plays at his high school football games, and his ability got better over time. Chris met my mother, Lucy McDonald, just one time, but he would always ask me about her by name ever after.

Byron's cardiologist, Dr. Phil Lobstein, once recounted an incident with him in his office.

On the way down the hall to the examining room, Byron noticed a photograph of the famed sixteenth hole at Cypress Point on the wall. He stopped, pointed that large forefinger of his at the picture and said with a gleam in his eye, "I birdied that hole in that match with Ben against Kenny and Harvie." Byron was eighty-seven years old then, and I was struck by the force of his comment, the strength and passion in his voice. It was the first time I realized the true level of his competitive zeal.

Maybe I'd been misled by the calm serenity of Byron's usual demeanor, but at that moment I knew I was in the presence of a great competitor. It suddenly became clear to me that this level of fiery emotion was what allowed Byron Nelson to achieve his greatness.

Please don't let anyone forget that while Lord Byron was ever the perfect gentleman, inside him was the competitive heart of a lion.

In contrast to that, Byron claimed one time that he couldn't memorize things, like poetry or song lyrics, even ones from his favorite musicals. So I challenged him on one of our five-hour drives to Kerrville, and he actually did memorize the Oscar Mayer bologna song. It was such a treat to hear this golf hero, revered by thousands, stop and sing those familiar words, ending with "Oscar Mayer has a way with B-O-L-O-G-N-A!" And then he'd look at me with that twinkle in his eyes and smile.

We also sang a sweet little love song called "Tell Me Why." Once we were taking my sister Joanie and her husband, Tom Howe, out to dinner. When we sang it to each other in the car, Joanie got tears in her eyes. Although the author is unknown, you may remember it from childhood:

> Tell me why the stars do shine,
> Tell me why the ivy twines,
> Tell me why the sky's so blue,
> And I will tell you just why I love you.

Because God made the stars to shine,

Because God made the ivy twine,

Because God made the sky so blue,

Because God made you, that's why I love you.

Byron the Artist

One talent Byron was absolutely positive he didn't possess was anything having to do with art—drawing, painting, and so forth. But he did get talked into a couple of ventures in this area, and the results were, well, interesting. First of all, our local Meals on Wheels organization asked if he would do a painting to be auctioned off at their annual golf tournament. So I helped by sketching a simple landscape and then mixed the colors and let him cover an 8" x 10" canvas. Doing that painting clearly was not his cup of tea, and when he learned later that someone paid $3,000 for it, he just shook his head and laughed. He did one more, this time for the Salesmanship Club, and when that one was finally finished (and brought in $2,600!), he said, "No more." Painting almost made him more nervous than teeing off at the Masters, I do believe.

One summer, though, our dear friend Marcia Baggs prevailed upon Byron to serve as a guinea pig for her. She had just taken a workshop with Dr. Betty Edwards on her technique called "Drawing on the Right Side of the Brain." Byron was absolutely the most reluctant student she ever had. Even so, when he began working on copying an upside down drawing by Picasso, he became so involved in it that he started going off the sheet of paper, and Marcia had to attach another one.

Finally, she said, "Okay, our time's up for today."

Byron said, "Wait, his tie's not right; I've got to fix it."

That sketch is now framed and hanging in Marcia's classroom at the new Byron Nelson High School in Trophy Club, Texas, just a few miles away from our ranch. To me it's more evidence of Byron's humility, that he was willing to try something very difficult, even though he didn't want to at all, just because we loved Marcia so much and he wanted to help her.

I Took You to Raise, Honey

Byron had such a sweet sense of humor that showed up at unexpected times, as with that Secretary's Day luncheon and the $25,000 lost whiskey endorsement. One of my favorite lines from him was when I would make a mess of things and become upset either with him or myself. When we'd had time to talk things over, and I would be down on myself, wondering why he even put up with me, he would laughingly say, "Don't worry, honey, I took you to raise." I always thought it was so caring, charming, and understanding of my considerable youth, compared to his longer life experience.

At the same time Byron was extraordinarily open to helpful criticism. Once when we had been married about a year, Byron was getting ready to leave for lunch in Dallas with friends. He was wearing a patterned gray-and-black sport coat that was no doubt very much in fashion when he bought it years before. But he hadn't been buying many clothes since well before Louise had her stroke, so to my mind the black medallion pattern on the gray looked a little old style. I didn't say anything then, just kind of *looked* at it the way only a wife can do, then kissed him good-bye and said I looked forward to seeing him later that afternoon. When he came home, the first thing he did was take off that sport coat and drop it on the floor, saying, "Give this away—I don't want to wear anything that you think doesn't look good." So instantly I was promoted to chief valet, and we both enjoyed the results.

Another time, when we had been at the Richland Hills Church of Christ for several years, I noticed that Byron checked his watch several times during the service, not because he was impatient or thought the singing or sermon was too long or short, but just because he noticed details like that. I was concerned that because people were so glad to see him there and talk with him they just might be noticing his every move and could get the wrong impression, so I suggested he might want to reduce his watch checking some. His reaction? "Then I just won't wear one to church at all—I don't need it anyway, and I don't want to give people the wrong idea."

Byron was also unusually conscientious about staying fit, and he never resisted going to the doctor for checkups when something needed attention. He would say, "I owe it to you to take care of myself as much as I can so you won't have to worry." So I never had to urge or fuss at him about his hips, hearing, or heart, and that was a blessing.

Having Our Boys

From the beginning Byron and my sons, John and Stan Tangeman, took to each other like cookies and ice cream, but in somewhat different ways. John, the older by one year and eight days, was already in love with golf and grew ever more so, while Stan, who had played golf before going off to college in Los Angeles, could take it or leave it. But Stan, who eventually acquired a master's in electronics engineering, bonded with Byron through his woodworking. He would spend hours in the shop helping Byron or building something on his own, and he learned not only a few things about Byron's hobby, but a lot about his stepfather's perseverance.

Stan came to visit several times before he found and married the amazing Hope. On one trip we were walking down the road together. I mentioned that Byron had said the day before that he was going to have to tear down one of the two large barns on the ranch. It was leaning at a rather desperate angle, and since it wasn't used much, it needed to be removed before someone got hurt.

Stan said, "He can't do that—I love that old barn!"

The upshot was that Stan went back to Los Angeles, did some research on restoring old barns, made a scale model of his plan, and sent us a proposal, including costs for materials, and he promised to rebuild it himself with help from two friends. Byron approved, and Stan and his buddies spent several weeks in our rainy, mosquito-infested spring working on the project. They really did a good job, too, because the barn is still standing, and Byron thoroughly enjoyed the time we all got to spend together. We have about a dozen or more funny stories that came from that experience, but it was worthwhile, even if it did end up with a little cost overrun and Stan's VW Vanagon getting flooded. The best part of all was when Stan's wonderful "friend," Hope Algarin, came to spend a few days, and my sixth sense told me, *This is who he's going to marry.*

Then there are John and Anne. John spent two years in art school before going to Boston with his rock and roll band to see how that would go. He met lovely, talented Anne at the Museum of Fine Arts, and they clicked right away. So Byron and I got to enjoy a couple of great fall-color trips and some golf with John and his buddies. Byron thought John had the fastest pair of hands in the golf swing he had ever seen—faster even than his great friend Chris Schenkel, who was legendary for how quickly he swung through impact. He knew John had a great love for the game and felt he had quite a bit of potential.

How much? Well, as the accompanying story shows, John came to Dallas one time, and we went to the golf course straight from the airport to play Cottonwood Valley. On the second hole he made a hole in one, which was so great because we were both there to see it. I do believe that was Byron's second favorite ace, next to the one I'd made in Florida years before. In fact, John's now about an eight handicap and is considering writing a narrative about his experiences playing all of the courses Byron played during that amazing year of 1945. Here's the story in John's own words:

I went to Dallas to visit my mother and Byron for a quiet weekend at their ranch. I brought my golf clubs, and after we left the airport, we thought it would be a great idea to play a quick nine holes at the Four Seasons. A mere thirty minutes later, I was with my mom and Byron on the first tee at Cottonwood Valley. And as many who have ever played golf with Byron know, it's quite intimidating to play golf with, never mind hitting your first tee shot with, the legend.

As usual I made double bogey on the first hole (I seem to do that every round, no matter where I'm playing). Then we came to the second tee, which is a little par three over water, about 145 yards from where I was. Playing as a young kid, I pulled out a nine-iron and proceeded to hit it thin. The nine-iron caught the ball about a dimple below the equator of the ball. Not only did I have a wrong club selection and hit the ball poorly, it somehow cleared the water, landed thirty yards in front of the green, and then rolled all the way into the hole some fifty yards from where it first landed.

"That's a hole-in-one!" Byron exclaimed.

It wasn't exactly how I'd had the shot drawn up, but there you have it.

The reason this is one of my favorite stories is not because I made a hole-in-one with Byron Nelson watching (and my mom, too), it was watching the simple joy Byron got out of playing with my mother. Although he could still hit the ball straighter and longer than I could, even at the age of seventy-six, he preferred to play from the forward tees with his beloved wife. So I made the hole in one, then watched as the two of them drove the cart down and teed off from the forward tees. It was about the cutest thing

I'd ever seen. The two of them were down there wishing each other luck and playing up to each other's competitive natures. It was then that I first saw true love.

A hole-in-one? So what. We should all be blessed to have what my mother and Byron had together for many years.

I did have Byron autograph the hole-in-one ball, however. I mean I'm not stupid. But whenever I look at that ball, the image that comes to mind is of Byron and Mom, playfully selecting clubs, teeing up their balls, and having the time of their lives being together in any and every moment.

Byron loved those two boys and always considered them his own sons. He also got such a kick out of being with them, and he loved watching how they related to each other and to me. Best of all, he became a grandfather five times because of John and Anne's sons, Finn and Reed, and Stan and Hope's boys, Floyd, Oliver, and Charlie. They made his life richer in ways he had never even expected.

About ten years ago, after both boys were married and at least one grandson had arrived, I was reading to Byron one evening just before we went to sleep from a devotional book by H. Norman Wright entitled *Quiet Times for Couples*. On this particular night we were asked to share something about our marriage that had enriched our own lives. My answer was that so many of Byron's friends being closer to his own age had taught me a lot of wisdom about how to look at life. When it was Byron's turn, he quietly said, "Having our boys." And that meant the world to me.

Dear Peggy,

Christmas is rapidly approaching, and this will be the first time in more than forty-five years that I won't be putting Byron's name on a card. . . I will try not to repeat all of the many nice things written and spoken after Byron's death. Having been a professional athlete, I judge other professional athletes with more than just a critical eye. I am totally unimpressed with all the 'hoop-la" and "halo adorning" that surrounds many of them.

Byron was in a class by himself. His unsurpassed golf achievements were immensely surpassed by his human qualities. He was gentle but tough; kind, considerate, and friendly without being overbearing. He was helpful to one and all, and always had time for those who sought his counsel. He was generous and fair, and all his life he was a contributor to the welfare of others. His faith in the Lord was rich and deep, and there was never any doubt in his mind that he would eventually be with his Lord forever.

Byron was blessed to have you as his companion during his later years. He reiterated over and over his love for you, and how grateful he was at having found you when he needed you most.

He was a remarkable human being who, at his departing, had not a single enemy. I was fortunate to have him as a friend.

Robert (Bobby) W. Brown, M. D.
Professional Baseball Player, 1946–52, 54
President of the American League 1984–1994, and
Byron's Longtime Friend
Written December 19, 2006

14

No Wonder They Call You "Lord"

It would be difficult to find a person who had less desire to write a book than Byron, yet he became the author of not one but three books (with help, as he would freely admit). Two of the books were instructional: *Byron Nelson's Winning Golf* (1946), and *Shape Your Swing the Modern Way* (1974). He also contributed forewords to several other authors' golf books.

When Byron was in his late seventies, friends had so often pleaded with him to get his wonderful stories and his life down on paper that he finally agreed to write the third book, with one condition—that I be the one to help him write it. I suppose I was somewhat qualified, having been an English major in college and an advertising writer for twelve years, but still, a whole book!

But it was so easy working with him, and I got to hear even more stories than I already knew by that time, including a couple he felt shouldn't be included in the book, which was titled *How I Played the*

Game. One of them was about his Grandfather Allen. As I was typing the manuscript one afternoon, I came across a reference to Mr. Allen, and I wasn't sure what his first name was.

Byron said, "Well, everyone called him Frank, but his full name was Moses Franklin Allen."

I looked at him, my eyes twinkling and said, "Your grandfather's name was Moses?"

Byron nodded, and I laughed, saying, "No wonder they called you 'Lord!'"

You might be wondering just how Byron came to be called "Lord Byron" in the first place. When Byron won the Masters in 1937, he was the youngest player ever to win it (just barely twenty-five) until Seve Ballesteros won in 1980. The Atlanta sportswriter O. B. Keeler, impressed by Byron's inspired, come-from-behind win on Sunday in the fourth round, wrote the headline for the papers the next day: "Lord Byron Wins the Masters." The reference was, of course, to the British poet George Gordon, who also held the title Lord Byron. Gordon had been competing with Napoleon Bonaparte for the love of Josephine, and when Napoleon won out, Gordon apparently got drunk and wrote a strongly worded poem attacking his rival over the affair, as well as Napoleon's defeat at Waterloo. So that is why Keeler applied the moniker to our Byron, and for whatever reason, it stuck, though in a quite different way than to Gordon, who died young from his various dissipations. Personally I've always rather enjoyed the fact that while Jack Nicklaus was called the "Golden Bear," and Arnold Palmer was called "The King," only Byron was called "Lord."

Another story concerned a pro he played against in the PGA

Championship finals one year. This player had a habit of jingling change in his pocket as Byron was getting ready to putt. Byron felt he shouldn't let it bother him, so he didn't say anything to the fellow. But as he said himself, while he played well throughout the match, he putted terribly and eventually lost. A good lesson for us all if something or someone is distracting us while we're trying to concentrate or win a major!

Another story Byron told our friends Roger and Joann Lehew was about when he was twelve years old and got his first golf club. They related Byron's story this way:

Another Mrs. Lehew—same name as ours and possibly related some way—lived on the same block as Byron's family. Byron would take that club and hit a golf ball down the road to and from school every day. Mrs. Lehew told Byron's mother to take it away from him before he broke every window on the street. Mother Nelson told her that Byron had good control of the club and the ball, but if he ever broke a window, he would pay for it. Needless to say, if that Mrs. Lehew had had her way, Byron might never have played golf at all!

Sidelights to the Streak

There are also a couple of interesting sidelights to Byron's 1945 streak. The first is that when Byron and Sam Snead tied at Charlotte and then tied again in the first eighteen-hole playoff (imagine a double eighteen-hole playoff when the prize money was only $2,000, and that was in war bonds!), Snead became upset about an article that appeared in the paper the next morning intimating that he had three-putted the last hole the day before on purpose so they could have another round and get more money from the gate receipts, which wasn't true in any case. Regardless, the article may have bothered Sam enough that he shot seventy-three the next day to Byron's sixty-nine. Had it not been for that article, Byron's streak might have ended right there.

You'll enjoy hearing Byron himself tell this story and many others from the famous winning streak on the CD included in the back of this book entitled *Byron Nelson Remembers 1945*.

Later on in the streak (win number seven as it turned out), Byron was teeing off on number thirteen in the final round of the Philadelphia Enquirer tournament when Leo Diegel came up to him and mentioned that Jug McSpaden had just shot sixty-six and was now leading Byron by several strokes. Byron knew he had to shoot five under par the remaining six holes to win, and he did it! He shot a sixty-three and beat McSpaden by one shot. But how did it happen that Diegel came out to tell Byron at just the perfect moment? You tell me!

Golf Can Be a Funny Game

Playing golf with Byron could be as intimidating for others as it was for me at first. Sometimes it was enough just to know Mr. Nelson was nearby to get folks rattled. One time we were waiting at the first tee at the TPC Four Seasons for our turn to tee off. Four men were ahead of us but hadn't hit yet, and they didn't know we were sitting about fifty feet behind them. Suddenly one guy turned around, caught sight of Byron, then eased over and whispered something to the others, who also turned around just enough to see The Hat.

The first guy took a great practice swing, and then sent his drive about fifty yards to the right. The second player went an equal distance to the left. The third, I think, topped his drive just off the front of the tee box, and the fourth sort of did a combination of all the above. You could see their embarrassment as they shuffled off to their carts and drove away as quickly as decency would allow, while Byron sat there with a surprised look on his face.

"My goodness," he said. "They looked like they could play better than that!"

Then there was his final round of charity golf. We had been married just a couple of years when he told me he had to go out to Preston Trail and fulfill an obligation to play a round of golf with three fellows who had won the prize in a local fundraiser. He didn't know any of them but was happy to do it, as he had done several times in the past for a variety of causes.

When he came home late that evening, he didn't have much to say for a while, but finally he told me some of the details. When he got there for lunch and sat down to visit with the men, he noticed an odd thing. All during the meal, not one of them asked him a single question about golf or the pros or the tour, which was unusual. So near the end of the meal, Byron said, "Well, let's get a little game up before we go out there, gentlemen. What are your handicaps?"

They all looked blankly at him and said, "What's a handicap?" That was when he knew it was going to be a strange afternoon.

As it turned out only one of them had ever played golf at all, and another had to borrow clubs from someone for the occasion because he didn't have any of his own. The lowest score anyone shot that day was 110, and that was if Byron didn't count the lost balls or the ones that went in the water. They wore out one forecaddie, who had to quit after nine holes because he had such terrible blisters from running hither and yon to rake traps and to find balls that had strayed into the woods. The blessing of all this was that these were fine Christian young men, so at least Byron didn't have to hear any poor language as they played, but it was quite a test of patience even for Lord Byron.

The next morning, as we were still snuggling in bed, Byron began chuckling and then actually laughing out loud. When I asked him what was so funny, he told me that the crowning touch on the whole day was when they were driving up to the clubhouse after the round and the gentleman in the cart with him said, "Mr. Nelson, I want you to know that when this comes up again next year, I'm going to make sure I buy it. This has been so much fun, and it was worth every penny of the two hundred and fifty dollars I paid for it!" Byron, recalling how previous such prizes had gone for a minimum of two thousand, didn't have the heart to tell him there wouldn't be any such prize next year. But that was the last charity round of golf he played, and it was worth every minute just because it provided him with a terrific story, the guys had a great time, and it apparently did the charity, whatever it was, at least a little good.

Peppy Lee Bueno: Another Dream Come True

Growing up as a city girl in Toledo, Ohio, my only glimpses of horses were as we would drive along I-75 to my uncle's home in Cincinnati for a visit. Even my grandparents' farm in Michigan didn't have any horses, and I had always thought they were the most beautiful animals in all of God's creation. I read every *Black Stallion* and other horse book I could find as a kid. So after Byron and I had been married about ten years, it occurred to me that with all these hundreds of acres and a barn already there, maybe I could have a horse of my very own.

My by-now-best-friend, Marcia Baggs, had already been teaching me the fundamentals of riding, using one of their several ranch horses, so I was all gung-ho. Marcia searched for several months and finally found Peppy Lee Bueno, a ten-year-old quarter horse gelding. As Byron and I went to look at him and watched Marcia, a superb horsewoman, ride him in the corral, I fell in love instantly with this handsome black horse, who, as Byron said later, "had kind eyes."

As it turned out Peppy certainly lived up to his name, and to catch him out in the pasture, I finally had to resort to bribing him with gourmet horse "cookies" made from oats, brown sugar, and apples. Either that or I had to chase him around in circles in 99-degree heat for about a half hour. Most of the times I rode, I would bring Peppy by Byron's woodshop so Byron could say hello. He really enjoyed seeing me ride, and it added an exhilarating new dimension to my life.

> Byron and Peggy loved our daughters so much that they eventually became the girls' honorary grandparents. Byron then decided to make us the offer that if the girls ever chose to attend a Christian college, he would pay the tuition. As it turned out, that wasn't Maeci's path, but Erin did select Abilene Christian University, and Byron lived up to his promise, which Peggy has continued to fulfill. He was a completely giving man and completely lovable.
>
> *Marcia Baggs*
> *Art Teacher, Byron Nelson High School*

When I wrote to our honorary granddaughter Maeci about this book, here's what she said:

For eighteen years Byron and Peggy made our lives so rich, so beautiful, I could not imagine a better childhood. The lessons I learned about family, love, God, and even golf over those nearly two decades changed me forever. No one else, aside from my sister, could say they had one of the most influential gentlemen in the world as their honorary grandfather, and that's how I know my stories of him are very special.

I miss him so.

In my mind, Uncle Byron is a collage of beautiful colors, an endless wheel that weaves itself into one beautiful story after the next. The experiences and lessons blend so tightly that asking for just one story is like pulling one string from a tapestry created over a lifetime.

I will never forget the holiday dinners at his table. Peggy always prepared the most fantastic meals, with a dining set that was fit for royalty. As we gathered around the table and talked, Uncle Byron listened to our schoolgirl stories as if they were the most important things in his life at that moment. He always bragged on Peggy (he loved her so much), telling her what a beautiful dinner she always made and what a fantastic cook, housewife, Christian, teacher, writer, singer, grandmother, friend—anything she did, he loved it with all of his heart. I always told him I would not settle for anyone who didn't love me as much as he loved Peggy.

One of my favorite stories about Byron was when he got his three-wheeled bicycle. He loved going on walks in the afternoon with Peggy, Erin, Mom, and me, so Peggy got this bicycle for him as a gift so that he could keep up. He rode it all over the ranch, this bright-red, adult-sized tricycle with a basket in the back. When Erin or I wanted to go with him, especially down the long driveway out to the mailbox, he would let us ride in that back basket. He would tote us like a chauffeur for princesses up and down the driveway. "Our job," he said, was "to hold on to the mail and keep it safe until we got in the house." I remember this being a daunting task, as my short, eight-year-old arms could barely wrap themselves around this massive pile of mail the golfing world sent for Byron to consult or sign. He always told us what a great job we had done when we got back to the house, acting as if he couldn't have gotten the mail without our help.

I do miss him so.

He was our biggest fan. When we would ask him how we could repay him for the fantastic gifts that he made us, he would always say, "You can repay me by giving to others anytime you can." So that's why I am writing this, because I think it is just one more way I can give a piece of Uncle Byron to others when I have the chance.

15

When Admitting a Mistake
Changed Lives

Byron's humble nature was a marvel in someone with so many accomplishments, but on one particular occasion, it made an enormous difference for two little girls from Russia and one from China. In 2003, shortly after the Colonial Invitational Tournament in Fort Worth, Byron received a letter from a man in Westlake, Ohio, near Akron. The letter began with a polite apology for "invading his privacy," but the writer said, "I thought you should know that something you said changed my life."

Naturally that got Byron's attention, and the man continued to tell his amazing story. When Matt Richardson and his wife, MJ, were unable to have children of their own, she wanted to adopt, but he was very cool to the idea. Then he picked up a golf magazine that featured an interview with Byron. The writer at one point asked Byron what was his greatest regret in life. Instead of saying he wished he had won the British Open or some other thing related to golf, Byron said, "When Louise and I couldn't have children, she wanted to adopt, but I didn't. And I realized, when it was too late, what a terrible thing I had done to her, because I know we would have been good parents and could have made some children happy."

The next thing young Matt Richardson wrote was, "Mr. Nelson, your words snapped me around. Since that time, we've made two trips to Russia and adopted Maria and Nadia, who are sisters. We realized very quickly that we did it not for ourselves, but for the girls. And it never would have happened except for what you said."

Byron and I were simply overcome, and a few months later, the entire Richardson family came to the ranch for a day. Those two little darlings ran all over the place, climbed fences, rode my horse Peppy, and had a ball. But the thing that touched me the most was hearing them say "Mama" and "Papa" to these two loving, courageous people who thought they would never get to hear those words.

Before they left, Matt gave Byron his own father's copy of Byron's book *Winning Golf* with the inscription, "Mr. Nelson, thank you for helping me create my family." What a remarkable couple!

Even more remarkably, when I shared their story with friends at church, it eventually resulted in another childless couple in somewhat the same situation adopting a sweet Chinese infant. When Byron got to see little Mei Ling one Sunday just a few weeks before he died, he smiled as they took his picture with her and held up three fingers, saying, "That's Number Three!" I know he never imagined that such a basketful of blessings could come from that one article, and we have delighted in telling these stories to all who would listen.

The Direct Approach

Other people have often described how Byron changed their lives as well. Our friend and general contractor, George Williams, tells this story:

> Byron and Peggy bought a house in town they wanted to remodel and sell and gave me the job of heading it up. Quite often during the several months that followed, Byron would drive up and say, "Just thought I'd come by and see what a good job you're doing." I always enjoyed those little visits with him; he was always encouraging and good to talk to.
>
> Then one day, he came and said, "George, come here a minute, I want to talk to you." I walked over to his car as always, but he said, "No, I want you to get in the car—I need to talk to you."
>
> Well that shook me up just a little, but of course I got in and he said, "The first thing, George, I want to thank you for—this is the husband in me—is how well you get along with Peggy."
>
> Then he continued, "George, you're a great guy. But you could be so much better of a person if you started going to church. I'm not asking you to go to *my* church, or even the Church of Christ, just go to church, because your life will be so much better if you do."
>
> I started trying to worm out of it as fast as I could, saying, "Byron, my only day off is Sunday, and I have things I have to do, and I'm tired and when I do go with Bronwyn I can't stay awake, the preacher's going too fast, and I can't find where he is in the Bible and . . . "

Then Byron began to tell me how, when he first started out on the tour and wasn't a very good player yet, he'd play on Sunday mornings and go to church in the evenings. Then as he got better and was leading in the fourth round, he'd have time to go to church in the morning and play golf later in the day. But either way he always made time for church.

It was only that one time he spoke so directly to me, but in other ways he just encouraged me to be a better person. I always enjoyed talking to him in his shop, though I didn't get to do it much. I did start to go to church more after that, but it wasn't until Byron and Peggy got me a good Bible with a thumb index, so I could find my way around it better, that I really started to understand it more. And it wasn't until after Byron died that I got to do some really serious Bible study with two very knowledgeable Christian men and finally got baptized. The neat thing was that it was the summer after I became a Christian that our son Kody did, too, when he was at Christian camp.

After Byron died, I repainted and organized his shop with Peggy's approval. She lets me use it for my office now, and that's a really special thing to me. I do my job estimates and bills there, and I have pictures of Byron to look at and remember him by. I was very blessed to know Byron. He changed my life.

My dear friend, Judy Stead, also talks about Byron's gift to her with this sweet story:

Of all the lessons learned from Byron, the one that impacted my life the most was that he taught me how to pray. Byron was my first encounter with a man of God. By that I mean one who has turned his life over to God in such a way that he witnesses his beliefs in all of his words and actions. So it was a wondrous thing to me to listen to this man pray. Byron's prayers were beautiful and spoken from the heart, always praising God, then requesting blessings for God's assistance in healing for friends and family and guidance for our leaders. He would conclude his prayer with an intercession to "guide, guard, and direct us." It was an awakening moment for me. The pattern of his prayers followed the pattern of the Lord's Prayer, and of course that was given to us so that we'd know how to pray. After Byron's prayers I did indeed feel blessed and protected.

Differences and Disasters

Even though Byron and I had a most unusual romance and wonderfully romantic twenty years together, it's important to tell you that Louise was not only his first love, but he loved her as truly and completely as he did me . . . and for thirty years longer. And while he praised her many accomplishments as his partner, homemaker, encourager, hostess, and cook, only one time did he ever say anything about our similarities or differences.

One day, I guess he had been turning over in his mind how the two of us lined up, and he said, "I'd always heard that when a man had a happy first marriage, if his wife died and he married again, he would marry a woman almost exactly like his first wife. But you and Louise couldn't be more different if you had come from different planets!" Probably the only things we had in common were that we both loved to cook, our favorite color was yellow, and we both simply adored Byron.

The Great Hummel Disaster

One of our differences was in the kinds of things we liked to collect. Actually, I would have to say I didn't really collect anything, per se, because I had never had the money to do it. But Louise loved beautiful things and had quite an array of American cut glass in the corner cabinets in the dining room. The cabinets had been specially built during some of their remodeling and had handsome glass doors, but there was no lighting inside, so you really couldn't see the cut glass pieces well. Eventually we put lights in the cabinets and replaced the wooden shelves with glass, which made all that gorgeous antique glassware sparkle like diamonds. We both felt Louise would have liked that.

In addition, Louise had accumulated about two dozen charming Hummel figurines. Considering how much she loved children and how disappointed she was that she and Byron couldn't have any, I imagine those little porcelains were very dear to her heart.

However, during her illness, after her death, and in the process of many dustings and cleanings, the Hummels had gotten out of position on the bookshelves in the den, which I knew bothered Byron some.

So a few months after the wedding, we set about reorganizing it all. Byron carefully showed me how to pound the shelf supports into the brackets with a couple of sharp taps of the hammer, and we got all the shelves redone and put everything back in one afternoon.

Byron went back out to his shop, and as I surveyed our handiwork, I decided the shelves the Hummels were on needed to be lowered a notch or two so people could see them better. Carefully I set all the figurines on a table, took the five-foot-long shelves down, lowered the supports, tapped them into the brackets with the hammer just as Byron taught me, put the shelves back, the figurines now displayed to their best possible advantage under the lights, and proceeded to make dinner for us. Some two hours later, as we were sitting there watching television, those supports sprang loose, the shelves flew off, and every one of those blessed Hummels hit the brick floor. It all seemed to happen in slow motion as Byron and I watched in stunned amazement from the other side of the room. We were both too far away to catch them, and every one was broken beyond repair.

Fortunately I'm not given to hysterics, but that would have been a good time for it. Byron's first concern was me, so he immediately said, "It's okay, sweetheart." Then he quietly went and got the broom, a dustpan, and a paper sack to put all the pieces in. He never said one word about why I didn't wait for him to help me, how upset Louise would have been, or how much those things meant to her.

The next morning he set the sack of broken Hummels out by the burn barrel near his shop, and in a little while his sister Ellen stormed into the shop and demanded to know why we had to smash all those Hummels. She no doubt had a pretty good idea of how much they were worth. Byron simply replied, "It's none of your affair," and went on with his woodworking.

When he told me that, I was aghast, realizing she could well have surmised I had pitched some kind of a fit and started flinging Hummels left, right, north, and south. So Byron did tell Ellen what really happened, thank goodness. I never did find out what those figurines were actually worth, which is probably just as well.

I got to play golf with Byron a few times, and while each experience had its moments, the funniest thing that happened was when I made a par, par, and birdie. Then Byron gave me a tip, and I went bogey, double bogey, triple bogey! Honestly my game would have collapsed without the tip (due to the law of averages and my average was a double bogey!), but I think he felt bad about it, though we laughed about it later.

Stanton Mark Tangeman
Peggy's Son, Byron's Stepson

16

The Master Craftsman

Byron began doing woodwork in 1976. His grandfather Allen had been a carpenter in Waxahachie, Texas, and had worked on several of the now historic homes in that charming city. Byron started with a recipe box for Louise and eventually made twenty-four more as Christmas presents for family and friends. Then there were luggage racks for the guest rooms (made from old church pews), wooden trivets for buffet tables, bread boards and cutting boards, round dining tables, and coffee tables modeled after his grandfather's old tool chest that he had restored years before from its rather dilapidated condition. He made one of these for Tom Watson's daughter Meg, one for his great-niece Nicole, and several others.

At first Byron didn't even have a real shop, but he got started using the two-car garage. Then he got the idea of fixing up a 16' x 44' former chicken barn near the house, and with Louise's approval the transformation was made. Now he had room for a ten-inch table saw, a drill press, and pretty much any other equipment he wanted and could afford. He truly loved woodworking, even though as he said, "Golf was easy for me. Woodworking is hard. But I love doing it—love the smell and the feel of the wood and the whole process of making something for someone, making Christmas presents."

Because woodworking was difficult for Byron, my high school cheerleading experience came in handy. Every so often my sweetheart would come in for lunch or a midafternoon break, and he'd just have made some dreadful mistake in the shop. He would be pretty downhearted and upset with himself, and my job was to encourage and praise and shower him with love, and he would get bucked up enough to go back, correct the problem, and eventually produce a wonderful piece.

The Byron Brand

One of the sweet things about Byron's love of woodworking was the friendships he made with professional woodworkers. One of them, Harris Edson in Kerrville, got to be good friends with Byron and surprised him with an electric branding iron using Byron's own autograph. My, but he was proud of that gift! After that he used it on every piece he made that was big enough to stamp with that beautiful signature of his.

His other favorite woodworker pal was Mark Gilger, who made custom furniture in Fort Worth. Whenever Byron was stumped about how to operate a new piece of equipment or what to do next on a project, he would call Mark and either go visit his shop or have him come out to the ranch. Byron felt so proud to call Mark and Harris his friends and was really surprised they wanted to help someone who was just an amateur. He treasured their friendship as well as their advice, and he never had any idea how much they admired him or why.

Byron preferred to make things people would and could use, not just whirligigs or decorative things, but things like end tables and storage chests, bud vases and magazine racks, doorstops and serving trays. Occasionally he would make really big pieces, including a hutch, coffee table, bookcase headboards, and chests of drawers for our dearest friends, Eddie and Marcia Baggs and their daughters Erin and Maeci. For our home in Kerrville, he made headboards, a ten-drawer chest of drawers, an enormous desk of six different kinds of wood—oak, mahogany, birdseye maple, cocobolo, walnut, and cherry—and a New England-style tack box of cherry and walnut.

Byron's masterpiece, the one of which he was proudest, was a six-foot-tall solid cherry bookcase that now stands in our upstairs hall. He had a great time making it, and because the plans were so clear and step-by-step, his craftsmanship was flawless, even though he had to scale it back more than a foot in both height and width. He got some help on how to do certain steps from Mark Gilger, but he did actually make every part of it himself. When he finished it I took a picture of him next to it in his shop, and he asked me to write a letter for him to the magazine where the plans came from to thank them for their excellent instructions. He soon received a nice letter back, though the editor didn't indicate he knew Byron was more than just another woodworker.

Someone at the magazine figured it out, though, because a couple of weeks later, he got a phone call saying they would like to send a photographer to take a picture of him with the bookcase and put it in their magazine. Byron was delighted, and when the photo appeared in the magazine in 1992 with the headline, "Nice shot, Byron!" he was almost more proud of that than winning any tournament in his career. After he died, the editors repeated that picture with a delightful article.

Byron also enjoyed the challenge of repairing things, such as chairs, tables, and just about anything made of wood. One time, as we drove past our church building in Roanoke, we saw someone had left an old oak partners desk outside. Asking around town we found no one who wanted it, so we took it home, and Byron set about thinking of what to do with it. We knew Maeci and Erin didn't have desks to do their homework on, so Byron figured out how to saw that huge thing in two, add legs and a new back and get both pieces stabilized and refinished. They're still there in the girls' rooms, and yes, they bear Byron's autograph.

When I was in elementary school I remember being asked to do a report on someone famous. I thought, *Uncle Byron must be pretty famous because people are always asking for his autograph.* So I went to him and told him what the assignment was and asked if I could do my report on him.

He said, "Well, Erin, you know I'm not really famous; I just have a lot of friends."

As I grew up I met more and more people who referred to him as their "friend." Even if they had only spent a few minutes with him, they left the conversation feeling they were friends. It was his kind and considerate spirit that made anyone who met him feel special and that he had a unique interest in them. And knowing him, I'm sure he did sincerely care for each person he met.

Erin Baggs
Honorary Granddaughter

Clocks, Swings, and Dizzy Spells

Although a master of his woodworking craft, Byron wasn't above making things from kits once in a while. One year he ordered a grandfather clock kit from a catalog. (We actually had a very handsome one in the living room, but it had never worked properly, Byron said. So we placed it in the entry hall more or less as a decoration.) The pieces and works for the new clock were all there, and the instructions were pretty easy to follow, but there were more than a hundred pieces of wood to fit together, sand, glue, stain, and varnish. It was quite a project, but the hardest part was following the instructions for getting it going. The instructions were in some sort of broken English, and it took more than two hours to get all the weights and chains and things in the right places. One thing we noticed was that one of the weights, probably for the minute hand, had to be hung on the correct side or it wouldn't work at all. It was significantly heavier than the other two, and once we got it all working and chiming, it occurred to me that the old granddad clock in the foyer might be having the same problem with the weights. So I checked, moved the weights around according to the new clock instructions, and lo, our Big Ben works perfectly now too!

Some years later Byron became more adventurous and ordered only the plans and inner works for a wall-hung jeweler's clock. It wasn't nearly as big as the grandfather clock, and things went along fairly smoothly until he started on the door. Something went wrong with the first effort, then with the second. Finally my frustrated husband quietly said, as he started on the third door, "If this one doesn't work, the whole thing's going in the burn barrel!" Fortunately his final effort turned out fine, and I admired him so much for his determination to complete the job that I had a little brass plaque made for it, reading, "Perseverance." Of course the scrap pieces from some of his projects created quite a bit of kindling, which we happily used in our fireplace in the cold weather. Can you imagine tossing a piece of walnut, cherry, or mahogany lumber into your cozy little hearth?

One time I asked Byron if I could buy one of his handmade wooden creations. A few weeks later a handmade wooden clock arrived at my door with a note from Byron saying it was a gift—no charge. That Byron Nelson wooden clock is my most prized possession.

Ted Purdy
Professional Golfer
2005 Byron Nelson Golf Tournament Champion

Something that required not only perseverance but also downright humility was our porch swing. Byron for many years was subject to the dizziness created by vertigo, and the motion of sitting in a swing was not to his liking. But I had asked him to make a porch swing for us several times, and we saw a terrific design for one at an outdoor furniture shop, so he decided to try it. It turned out wonderfully— nice and substantial with a curved back and seat. Best of all, when Byron realized that the person with the longest legs controls how much you swing, he was quite content to sit in ours with me, and we spent many a pleasant hour doing just that. In fact, after he finished ours at the ranch, he followed it with one for our vacation home in Kerrville (which the new owner, our friend Julia Finger, gets to enjoy now), one for our Kerrville neighbors Ross and Margaret Collins, one for Eddie and Marcia Baggs, and, finally, one for his great-niece, Nicole Youngblood. I thought that was quite an accomplishment for someone who doesn't like to swing!

Byron was really plagued by vertigo for more than forty years. It would come about once a month and make him fairly miserable. His way of getting rid of it was with a couple of big doses of milk of magnesia. Even between the serious bouts of dizziness, he would sometimes say that his balance was off, and for a man who never lost his balance on a golf shot, that was most disturbing to him.

By chance one day I saw part of a television ad for a magnesium supplement product called Slo-Mag. Since I had always wondered why the magnesia liquid helped Byron, I looked it up on the Internet. It didn't say it was for vertigo, but it did mention that men need 400 mg of magnesium per day, while women need 320 mg. That intrigued me enough to look on our bottle of milk of magnesia, and wonder of wonders, it said the adult dose held 400 mg of magnesium!

I raced to the store and found Slo-Mag, and once Byron started taking it on a daily basis, he was never bothered with vertigo or loss of balance again. It was such a joy and comfort to both of us to be finished with that particular nuisance, though I must add that before, even when Byron was in the throes of an attack, he would still get up and go to work in the shop or at his desk. He would say that he felt worse lying down anyway, because vertigo was the worst a person could feel without actually being sick. Now the additional magnesium probably won't help everyone with vertigo, because there are several different problems that cause this disorder, but it surely helped my wonderful husband!

Byron wanted to learn how to be the best woodworker he could be, just like he wanted to be and was the best golfer. His goal was to be the best he could be in whatever he was doing.

The first time he came into our shop, Kerrcrafters, and asked if he could speak to the owner, I went to my dad in the back of the building and told him there was some guy who wanted to talk to him. Having no knowledge of golf, not only did I not know he was Byron Nelson, but I didn't even know who Byron Nelson was.

One time Byron asked my father to honestly grade him on the work he did on a storage chest he'd built. Dad gave him a B, and Byron immediately asked what he could have done to get an A. And Dad told him!

Pat and Judy Edson
Kerrville Woodworking Friends from the 1980s

Mishaps in the Shop

In our own home, there are numerous pieces of Byron's handiwork besides the grandfather clock, such as a barrister's bookcase, ottomans, several small side tables, my own office desk, an oak filing cabinet, a mahogany serving tray, mahogany shelving units, a dictionary stand, mahogany bench for the foot of the bed in our master bedroom, a cherry corner desk in the guest room, headboards for the beds in the upstairs bedroom, and a handsome oak kitchen stool.

Even though Byron never pretended to have an engineering mind, he was almost as good at figuring out woodworking challenges as he was at helping people with their golf swings. Our CPA and good friend, Jon Bradley, discovered a beautiful antique, illustrated family Bible inside a grocery sack in a closet of his parents' home after they had passed away. After he'd had it restored, he asked Byron to make a display case for it, and Byron agreed. He puzzled over how to do it for quite a while, but he finally produced a piece with glass on three sides and in the lid, which Jon could raise up to look at or remove the Bible. It was a nifty accomplishment, even for a guy with five golf records.

I could spend pages and pages listing every item Byron made, large and small. One time, after we had been married about fifteen years, we began to add up all the things he had made through the years, including Christmas presents he produced on a kind of assembly line, twenty-four or more at a time. At that point we figured he had done more than 450 pieces. And that doesn't include the chairs, tables, and other pieces he had repaired for folks. It really was wonderful to see how much enjoyment he got from this absorbing hobby.

His favorite type of wood to work with was Honduras mahogany. He loved the grain and feel of it, and it took stain very evenly, plus he could finish it lighter or darker according to who would be receiving it. He also used cherry, walnut, and oak, and once in a while something more exotic like cocobolo, cardinal wood, or wenge. We were both surprised to learn that some tropical woods are actually quite toxic, so if he used those, he would have to wear a mask and have good ventilation when he was sanding or sawing them.

Woodworking is a great pastime, but it does have a downside of danger, much more than playing golf. Byron's first mishap was on an afternoon when our paperhangers were installing wallcovering in our bedroom. David Kirby asked Byron if he would make a board with a slot on the top to fit on Dave's ladder so he could put his trowel there where it would be more convenient. Byron figured it would be an easy job, and it would have been fine if he had been just a wee bit more cautious.

Knowing we needed to get ready to go the Fort Worth rodeo that night, he decided not to use pushers to hold the board down when he cut the slot. The table saw grabbed the board from his hands but took part of his middle finger with it. I was in the office when he came in with his hand held up in the air and a rag wrapped around it.

"Honey, would you call Dr. Murphy at the golf course and ask him to meet us at his office? I've cut my finger and I'll need some stitches."

I called Rivercrest Country Club in Fort Worth and asked the pro to get the message to Dr. Murphy, hung up, and turned around to ask Byron, "How badly did you cut it, honey?"

"I cut the whole first joint off."

Oh my.

I picked up the phone again, called the pro shop, and I said, "Please tell Dr. Murphy to meet us at the emergency room at All Saints Hospital instead."

So we got in the car, and I made the twenty-two-mile trip in twenty-seven minutes, with Byron working hard not to pass out. The hand surgeon met Dr. Murphy and us, and he gave Byron a nerve-blocking shot immediately. After an hour or so of surgery, he was all fixed up, and we got back in the car, which was when I went to pieces just a bit.

Byron said, "We can still go to the rodeo, honey, if you want to."

I replied, "I don't think so."

We stopped at a drugstore on the way home to get his pain prescription filled, and while I was waiting, I picked out a get-well card that said, "Heard about your accident . . . Way to go, klutz!" When I gave it to Byron later, he had just enough humor left to laugh and say, "That's just what I deserve!"

His finger was saved, though it was then straight at the end and got in his way at times, but it was a good reminder to be more careful, which he tried hard to do. However, over the next few years, there were a couple more trips to the emergency room. After the fourth injury, we agreed that his helper, Manuel Marquez, who had lived and worked at the ranch for ten years by then, would operate the dangerous machinery. That included the table saw, band saw, radial arm saw, and anything else that made a lot of noise and was designed to cut wood, not fingers.

Byron was so good about it, accepting that time and circumstances necessarily limited his abilities in this area as well as in golf. But he still loved making small end tables, clocks, and even an oak transition piece in the doorway of our kitchen. It has his autograph on it and pleases me every time I step across that threshold.

Goodness in Action

One of the most charming things Byron would say when asked about his woodworking was, "I'm not a wealthy man, but when I ruin a board, I've got enough money to go out and buy another piece to replace it."

Byron's most unusual quality was his godly humility. He taught us that greatness can be surrounded by modesty and kindness, and his active zeal for service to God and his fellow men did not wane as he aged. Although Byron was a celebrity, he was always well-focused spiritually as a Christian. We think fondly of him every time we look at the lovely little wooden clock he made for us that sits in our kitchen window.

Jon and Joan Jones
Former Senior Pulpit Minister and Wife
Richland Hills Church of Christ

Byron was sometimes asked if he would make things to sell, but he never wanted to do that. One time he was prevailed upon to donate one of his small clocks for the PGA Tour Wives' charity event during our tournament. When he heard it had sold for $700, his comment was, "Well, some folks have more money than sense, don't they?" But he was glad the money went to a great cause.

Probably the best-known person he ever gave one of his end tables to was Phil Mickelson and his lovely wife, Amy. It was solid mahogany, and Amy told me that they had it surrounded by pillows and covered with blankets on the plane on the way back to San Diego. So I guess you could say they liked it.

He also gave one of those end tables to our preacher, Rick Atchley, and his wife, Jamie. We had been to their home once for a church event, and Byron noticed that Rick didn't have a convenient place to put his iced tea when he was watching television. So he got busy the next day, and a week later we brought it over to Rick and Jamie's house. It was simply Byron's way to notice things like that and want to help, to do something about it. Goodness itself.

Perhaps the piece he was proudest of next to the six-foot bookcase was the New England tack box, made for holding saddles, bridles, boots, and other items for grooming a horse. We saw a picture of one in a catalog, and it was so handsome that even though we didn't have a place for it right then, Byron was just so excited about the challenge of making it, he simply "got right after it," as we say in Texas. He showed the picture to his woodworking buddy in Kerrville, Harris Edson, who drew up the plans for it on his computer. Then Mark Gilger, his other woodworking expert in Fort Worth, helped him figure things out when he would get stuck. Between the three of them, Byron produced a very handsome cherry and walnut trunk that now graces our master bedroom, and since the three guys all worked on it, I had a plaque made and engraved with the word "Harmony." That says it all.

17

Wait, This Guy's in Terrible Trouble!

Growing up in Ohio in a blue-collar family of five kids without much money to spare for entertainment, one thing that was easy for me to do (and free) was reading. We had a good public library within walking distance, so I hied myself there every week or so to get more books. I simply loved to read. That's where I discovered *The Black Stallion; Lad: A Dog;* and many other great stories. One summer, I actually read fifty-six books. Later I came upon the British humorist P. G. Wodehouse, a writer who could make me laugh until I cried, especially with his golf stories.

As I mentioned earlier, when I first met Byron, I thought he would enjoy some of those golf tales as much as I did, so I sent him Wodehouse's *Golf Omnibus.* At the time I didn't know he really didn't enjoy reading about golf, but he would pore for hours over woodworking catalogs and magazines. It made me a little sad that he had never learned to read just for the fun of it.

One day we stopped in Clifton on our way home from Kerrville to visit James and Mary Ellen Boren. James was a wonderful Western artist and a fine Christian, and he showed us some of the books he used for inspiration for his art. Many of the books were by a writer named Louis L'Amour, and I figured if they were okay for James, Byron might like them, too, so I bought him a couple. If you've ever read any of L'Amour's works, you know you're hooked by the end of the first paragraph, because his stories are action-packed and just plain fun.

It wasn't long until Byron would be so deep into one of those novels that when I called him for lunch or dinner, he would say, "Wait a minute, this guy's in a terrible fix; I've got to get him out of trouble!" It was delightful to see him reading for pure entertainment, and the stories were so clean and with just enough romance in most of them that I got hooked myself.

Byron's Favorite Book

Byron did get great satisfaction and strength from an entirely different type of reading, though, and that was his Bible. His favorite Bible books were Proverbs, Psalms, and the gospel of John. He would re-read them every so often, sometimes sharing passages aloud with me. We also read a devotional at night when we were in bed, usually just one page from a book like H. Norman Wright's *Quiet Times for Couples* or Charles Spurgeon's *Morning and Evening*.

Byron liked for me to read aloud to him. Since I'd just discovered the Anne of Green Gables series at this late stage in my life, I would read a few pages of L. M. Montgomery's works to him each night.

He really enjoyed them and marveled at how the author could make those youngsters seem so alive and real. It was such fun to share things like that with him, because he had a gift for appreciating talent in others and always seemed to think that their accomplishments far outshone his own. Silly guy.

As a tactical officer for the city of Irving, I provided dignitary protection for Byron and Peggy approximately six years during the Byron Nelson golf tournament.

From the moment I walked into the headquarters trailer and met Byron, I could tell he was a very special person. I had never met anyone in my life who commanded so much respect but expected none. Meeting Byron for the first time was an unforgettable moment in my life, because he could make you feel like the only person in the room and that we had been best friends forever. He was the first person I had ever met who had that quality about him.

I remember how he constantly reminded me of how important his personal relationship with Jesus Christ was in his life. Byron told me that without Jesus he would have nothing. Byron was more than words; he was all action. He led by example. I hope I can say that knowing and loving Byron Nelson made me a better husband, father, and most importantly, a Christ-follower.

Rick Cutler
Sergeant, Irving Police Department
Byron's Personal Bodyguard 1999–2006

Love and Laughter

One of the ways Byron showed his appreciation for others was his wonderful laugh. He appreciated humor and good jokes, and I enjoyed saying things that tickled his funny bone. Coming from a family with a pretty off-the-wall wit, it was natural for me to look at life in an offbeat kind of way, and Byron had his own sense of humor, so we laughed together a lot through the years. In fact, Byron told me more than once that he had laughed more in the time we had been married than he had in the whole seventy-five years before that. Quite a nice compliment! I think there were also times he was laughing inside and not letting me see it, because I so often did goofy things or fussed about some small irritation, and he knew it was in his best interest not to let me know he sometimes found my little hissy fits amusing.

One evening we were on the way home from Dallas driving down a narrow two-lane street, and I was driving behind a man who was going even more slowly than the law allowed. I was grinding my teeth at the slowpoke for several blocks, no doubt coming close to the dictionary definition of tailgating, when suddenly the car turned into an alleyway in the middle of a block. In frustrated surprise I said, "Well, why did he do that?"

Byron's quiet reply was, "I think he was just trying to get out of your way!"

Point taken.

Regarding that issue of my driving habits, about a year after we were married we were driving to Dallas, and out of the blue I asked Byron, "What do you think I should work on to become a better person?" I was actually astonished to hear these words coming out of my mouth, because I was such an independent twerp I had never asked anyone for advice before.

Here was the wise man's answer: "Well, honey, I love you just the way you are. But since you asked me, I think you'd be happier with yourself if you could be more patient with other drivers."

That struck me as such plain common-sense wisdom that I chewed on the idea all the rest of the way to town. I found the change not only easy, but also quite beneficial to me, my passengers, and untold numbers of other unsuspecting drivers.

Mr. Romance

There were moments in our nearly twenty years together when I would fall far short of Byron's or even my own standards of patience, perseverance, and several other virtues. When I would wonder aloud to him about how he managed to put up with me, or what he saw in me in the first place, he would sometimes say, "I saw what you could be." Isn't that amazing? He had such a gift for not only seeing the best in people but helping them, often in some unspoken way, to bring it out, and to become better people just because they had been around him, even for a little while. You're beginning to see, I think, why I have always felt that I'm an extraordinarily blessed woman.

Byron was such a generous, giving person with everyone, but especially with me. He loved giving me jewelry, as most husbands do, but he was wisely hesitant about buying clothes for me, knowing we females have mysterious tastes in that area. Then as time went on, and it became too difficult for him to go with me to a mall or even to a large department store, we fortunately hit on a perfect solution. Being well supplied with dozens of catalogs, it became my habit to go through my favorite ones and circle items I liked but wouldn't necessarily order for myself. Then I'd specify what size, color, and style I needed and put the page numbers on the front of each issue. These would go into a special file in Byron's desk drawer, and whenever he got the urge to treat me, whether it was a birthday, anniversary, or "just because," he'd pick out one of those circled items that he liked as well, and order it. That way I would always be surprised, and it would already be something I liked. Plus, if it didn't fit or wasn't satisfactory somehow, it certainly wasn't his fault! Even more fun for me was surprising Byron with something really special. It might be a large piece of woodworking equipment, satellite TV dish, or a bronze statue of a caddie to decorate our entry drive. In every case I would manage with help from Eddie and Marcia to get the thing into Byron's shop, complete with red bow on top, or placed appropriately on just the perfect birthday, Father's Day, or whatever.

The two best surprises of all were his silver Masters cigar box and his E-Z-GO golf cart. The Masters box was given to Masters champions beginning in 1960, but wasn't retroactive, and Byron had mentioned occasionally that he sure would like to have one. So I asked permission, and since I paid for it, permission was granted. The box was created by Garrard's of London (silversmiths to the Queen, no less!), shipped to Texas, and when I presented it to Byron for our fifth anniversary, he was so delighted he was speechless.

On the practical side, the golf cart was even more of a blessing. After two hip surgeries, the only way Byron could comfortably get to his shop, a hundred paces from the house, was in his car. Plus he also wanted to accompany me on my walks in the afternoons when no one else was around, and the car didn't work so well for that.

The wonderful people at E-Z-GO, whose products Byron had always promoted just out of the goodness of his heart and for no compensation whatsoever, had supplied him with a special cart for his tournament every year. So at my request, one day Bill Tanner secretly brought out to the ranch this beautiful bright red golf cart with Byron's signature on the front. Eddie hid it in the hay barn until after Byron and I left for church on Father's Day, then he put it in our garage—once again complete with a huge red bow. When we returned from church, it was sitting right there as the door went up, and I announced, "Happy Father's Day, sweetheart!" Byron not only used that cart every day for the next five years, but he often said it truly was the best gift I ever gave him.

One of the most wonderful signs of Byron's love was something he did for our second anniversary. Unbeknownst to me he had gone out to Preston Trail, where there was a display of some of his medals and other small mementos, and asked if he could replace the 1937 Masters Gold Medal with another one he had. They cooperated, fortunately, and he then took that precious piece of history to our jeweler, had it made into a beautiful pendant, and gave it to me. It truly brought tears to my eyes, because I knew that was the most important tournament in his career to him, so I understood how much it signified of not only his love for me but also his trust that I could prove worthy of such a gift.

You may wonder what our days and weeks and months and years together were like. We quickly developed a comfortable pattern of normalcy. When we were at home, we had breakfast together, and then Byron would do the dishes and go out to his shop for some woodworking. He would come in later for lunch, then go back to the shop or maybe to play golf with friends in Dallas or Fort Worth. We typically had a fairly early dinner and relaxed in the evenings together. At first I remember Byron had been so used to going to bed early while Louise was ill that he thought 9:30 was about the right time to go to sleep. But he had also been used to getting up at 5:30 or 6 a.m. to take care of Louise. Fortunately, we were soon able to change that schedule by a couple of hours.

Soon after we celebrated our one-month anniversary, Byron announced his next goal was to make it to one hundred months, which we gleefully celebrated with an elegant dinner at the Four Seasons. The monthly anniversaries continued until we got to ten years, then he wanted to get to two hundred months, which we did. Each month was sweeter than the one before, until finally, just eleven days before he went to heaven, we celebrated number 238 at the Olive Garden, another of our favorite restaurants. How we delighted in each other!

When we were driving to Dallas, Fort Worth, Kerrville, or wherever, we held hands. Byron's were always so warm, and of course, if you ever got to shake hands with him, you knew his hands were really big. In fact, when we were first married, his grip on mine as we drove along would slowly, gradually, get tighter and tighter until I would need to shake mine a little bit to restore the circulation. One time when I did that, he apologized and said, "I guess I'm trying to make sure you're not going to go back to Ohio." Fat chance.

As everyone who knew Byron well would agree, he was a born encourager. He found ways to express his appreciation and enjoyment of others and did so at every opportunity. Above the other compliments from him, my very favorite was when he would say, "When you look at me, your eyes sparkle and dance!" It said so much about the feeling that flowed between the two of us. He really did light up my life so beautifully that it was the most natural thing in the world to reflect that light right back to him. I always had the same reaction when we had been separated even for as little as an hour at church, if I was helping with a children's class while he was in the adult Bible study. When I would catch sight of him again, my heart would beat faster, and I'd say to myself, *There he is!*

We had so many pet names for each other that some folks might find it a bit silly, but we enjoyed and used every single one: Honeypot, Queen of All Queens, Sleeping Tiger, Adorable Darling, Angeldoll, Cuddlebear, and the like. And of course, on a more formal note, we occasionally addressed each other as Mr. Nelson and Mrs. Nelson just for the sheer joyful fun of it.

I felt so secure, so completely cherished and appreciated in every way with Byron. His praise of my every little accomplishment, or sometimes just the way I walked, was unceasing. It occurred to me that, if we could only hear what God is saying to us, it would be like that too—constant praise and gentle guidance when we needed it. Or occasionally it might be a more pronounced "No!" when a temptation gets a little too strong for us to handle by ourselves.

Byron once said to me, "You are no better and no worse than any man you meet. We are all creatures of God and share the same world. In life and in golf, focus on your next shot, not the one you just hit or the shot you hit last week or last year. Also, be sure your next shot—in golf or in life—will result in being in a better position than you are right now." He was the closest man I ever met to being Christlike.

James A. Murphy, MD
Family Doctor and Friend

18

Winning the Final Round

Byron always had trouble understanding why anyone wanted his autograph, though he was glad to oblige. In 2000, when the Salesmanship Club was working on the cover art for the tournament program and asked us to supply a quote from him to be part of the artwork, we came up with this one: "I never thought I was any different from or better than anyone else just because I played a little golf over fifty years ago. But people treat me that way, and all I can do is be grateful and try hard to deserve it."

It's always been one of my favorite sayings of his because it so truly shows his lack of false pride as well as his lifelong effort to live up to the highest possible standard. Tom Watson once quoted Byron as telling him, "It's not how you play. It's how you conduct yourself and how you treat people."

Since Byron didn't understand why people wanted his autograph, he thought the only reason his name was on the tournament each year was because it would bring more golf pros to Dallas. He also didn't count on having streets named for him, like the one-mile stretch in his beloved Roanoke, or Byron Nelson Boulevard in Southlake that goes to the entrance of Timarron Country Club, whose golf course he helped design, or Byron Nelson Way that runs by the Four Seasons Resort in Irving next to the TPC tournament site.

But when the talk began about a Congressional Gold Medal in his honor, Byron really did think at least a few people had gone off their rockers. He thought that an award for humanitarian service such as this one should go to people who had given many millions or even billions of dollars to some great cause like eradicating hunger or eliminating poverty in some underdeveloped country. But the people around him were very much aware that Byron's whole life was about giving to and serving others in any way he could. And as most of us realize, it's a lot easier to write a check than it is to spend hours and

My mother once proclaimed, "Byron is the greatest man to ever take a golf swing." Growing up just a few miles from his ranch home in Roanoke, I frequently heard of his accomplishments. His humanitarian works became known to me only much later. However, as we worked on the Congressional Gold Medal award it became clear that his greatest work occurred off the golf course. The innumerable lives he touched and improved will remain a living legacy to the greatness of the man.

—*Congressman Michael Burgess*
Nominated Byron for Congressional Gold Medal

days and weeks in actual service to others. Byron did both, and he did a lot of it, more than even he realized.

The final honor, to him in some ways even more important than the Gold Medal, was having a new high school named for him in Trophy Club. It's an extraordinarily handsome building and everyone there is truly excited about having this gentle hero as their namesake. The students, who were given the task of coming up with the school motto, colors, and team nickname, were quite taken with one particular quote from Byron, "A winner is a different breed of cat." Thus we'll be cheering the Byron Nelson Bobcats in every competition and sport. It's very appropriate, too, because the school campus is on the edge of Grapevine Lake property, and bobcats are native to the area.

More Medical Adventures

After Byron's hernia repair shortly after we were married, there was a four-year interval when we were both healthy as could be. But my sweetheart had begun limping a little, and it became more and more noticeable. At first he would say, "It's just a little hitch in my get-go," but soon it was more pain than a hitch, so his left hip was replaced in 1990. Unfortunately, it didn't take and had to be redone in October of 1991, shortly after our return from Japan for the golf course project he was working on there. The stress of the hip pain, the travel, and probably just living with me brought on an attack of shingles on his shoulder, but the doctor recommended big doses of l-lysine and, happily, that went away.

Unfortunately, there was a complication with the second hip

replacement, resulting in a third-degree burn and a skin graft. Did he complain? No. Did he consider suing the doctors who had messed up? No. Was he happy about it? No. But gripe he would not, accepting the situation as gracefully as he did when winning or losing a golf tournament, and life went on.

Between Byron's medical adventures, I had one of my own. In the fall of 1998, I realized one night, just before dropping off to sleep, that a lump in my left breast had changed from the softness it had had several months before to a hard mass, like a large stone about two inches across. Somehow I knew it was cancer, but I didn't say anything to Byron. Instead I just set up doctors' appointments on my own, had a needle biopsy, and when the results came back positive, I told Byron that it was my turn for surgery. The doctors determined my best chance was a mastectomy and something called a TRAM flap. I remember sitting in the plastic surgeon's office, watching the assistant as she demonstrated what was going to happen, using a cloth doll with zippers in all sorts of places, and as I was mesmerized by it all, I suddenly realized, "I'm going to have a vacation! I get to lie around and read and take naps and everybody has to take care of me!"

Byron wasn't quite so sanguine about it, but he never let me see he was worried. He just continued being positive and optimistic, and as a matter of fact, he was right. I never had any post-op pain, though healing from this fairly major operation took awhile; but I got up the day after I came home from the hospital and went for a slow but steady half-mile walk, bent over as if I was ninety-nine years old instead of fifty-five. Increasing that bit by bit, within a week I was walking two miles and getting my energy back.

Following that came reconstruction, reduction, and other fascinating diversions, but I actually felt I was blessed by all the caring, wonderful people at All Saints Hospital and the several doctors who took care of me. In fact, Dr. Murphy, when he came to see me the morning after the surgery, said, "You look a lot better than I was afraid you'd look!" That made me laugh and brightened my day considerably.

My only setback was that after the surgery, I was told that although the cancer hadn't spread, I still needed to have four adjuvant chemo treatments. That did kind of get to me, because I had heard plenty about chemo making people sick, and I didn't care for that idea. So that one night my brave resolve weakened a bit, and Byron held me so tenderly in his arms as I cried, "I don't want to be sick; I don't want to see any more doctors!"

As it turned out, Dr. Mary Milam was not only a wonderful oncologist, she was highly regarded in her specialty and a woman I genuinely enjoyed getting to know. I did play a little trick on her, though. On our first visit, when she asked if I had any questions, I said, "When I get through with all the surgery and chemo, will I be able to play the violin?"

She thought for a minute, held her arms up in the position of a violinist with an imaginary Stradivarius on her shoulder, and said, "Yes, I think so."

With a straight face, I said, "That's funny . . . I never could before." Right then, poor Dr. Milam knew she had one of her more unusual patients!

Here's the best part about it all: when the chemo had its usual effect and my hair came out, I wore a wig during the day whenever we were

> I'd like to think I was a good friend to Byron. I cleaned his and Peggy's home for ten years before his passing. I've never met anyone like him, or the way he showed such loving care for his wife Peggy. When she was recovering from cancer surgery, he was always there by her side to help. Sometimes, he wanted to do something for her but she didn't want anyone to help, and it was the first time I saw him cry, because he wanted to help her so much.
>
> Byron and Peggy's marriage was like the first day they got married—they were always newlyweds and that is how it should be for anyone who's married. It was like a personal relationship with God forever and ever.
>
> *Jean Ossowski*
> *Housekeeper, Friend, and Fellow Christian*

out shopping or whatever. But in the evening, that thing would get a little itchy and annoying, so I would usually whip it off and fling it across the room. Do you know what Mr. Nelson would say?

"Sweetheart, I've always loved the shape of your head, and now I can see how beautiful it really is."

Really! He actually said that and meant it, and it made all the difference in the world to my little carved-up, stitched-up, bald ego. What a blessing to be married to such a man, such a loving friend and dear companion!

Ninety and Still Champ

In 2004, when Byron was ninety, his lower back had become more troublesome than even he could tolerate. After some searching we found a doctor in Dallas at the University of Texas Southwestern

Medical Center who was willing to do the surgery. When he came to talk to me afterward, Dr. Morgan said, "I don't like to work on celebrities, but when I opened up Byron's back, he had the muscles and bones of a man of sixty instead of ninety, and it was a piece of cake." So my champion once again came through with flying colors!

Finally his right hip was replaced, thankfully with no complications, and for a while he was still able to play golf from time to time. All told there were about a dozen hospital stays for one reason or another, and that wonderful strong heart of his just kept going and going. Finally, though, even it needed some additional help from a pacemaker and then oxygen during the night.

One of my sweetest memories came that second-to-last Christmas season, when our son John in Seattle had begged me to come see the *Nutcracker* ballet at the theater where he worked as audience services manager. He said that Anne, Finn, and Reed really wanted me to come too. Byron felt it was important and urged me to go, so I got our dear friend Linda Leveridge to stay with Byron, took off for a very fast one-night trip, had a great time at the performance and seeing the boys and John and Anne, then raced home. As I came from the garage into the office, there was my handsome sweetheart, standing at the counter and smiling big as the sun, with both arms wide open to fold me in. It's a picture I carry with me every day, and someday I'll see him again just like that, welcoming me home at last and for always.

Once Byron was on oxygen full-time, I guess we both knew he wasn't going to make it to the century mark, but neither of us spoke about it. I didn't ask the doctors for a prognosis because I thought it might make me treat him differently, like an invalid or something, and I didn't want that to happen. We got him a scooter that was a great help, portable oxygen supplies, and his golf cart helped him get to and from his beloved woodshop right up until the day he went to heaven.

I'm So Glad You're In Heaven Now

One of the strange things about the day Byron died was that he felt absolutely fine that morning. In fact he had slept better the night before than he had in several weeks. So we both got up at our usual 7:00 a.m. so we could finish breakfast in time to listen to Alistair Begg's *Truth For Life* radio program at 8:30. We showered, dressed, had Byron's favorite breakfast of a sausage biscuit, scrambled eggs, fruit, juice, and coffee with cream. Then Byron began doing the dishes just as usual while I got ready to go to my ladies' Bible class.

As I walked through the den and the office heading out to the garage, I asked if he would like for me to turn on the radio on his desk so he could listen to Alistair before he went out to his shop. He said yes and that he would turn the radio off before he went out. So we kissed good-bye, and he said, "Sweetheart, I'm so proud of you." He loved that I was helping to teach one of the ladies' classes and knew it required quite a bit of extra preparation on my part each week.

After class was over, I called Byron on my way home and left a message: "Hello, my adorable darling! I'm on my way home. Can't wait to see you and have lunch with you! I love you so much. Bye!"

When I pulled into the driveway, I saw Byron's E-Z-GO golf cart at the back door, and I figured he must have just come back in from the shop. I came in, carrying a box of doughnuts I had picked up earlier at Price Doughnuts in Keller, but he wasn't in his office. His car was in the garage, so I knew he was on the ranch somewhere. *Maybe he's in the restroom,* I thought, and decided to take the doughnuts to the kitchen and get started on lunch.

When I didn't hear him coming on his scooter, I went looking for him. He wasn't in the restroom, so I opened the door to where his golf cart was sitting outside and found my precious love lying there on the small back porch, stretched out very peacefully as if he was asleep, with his head resting against the outside wall.

From his lack of color, I knew immediately he was dead and had been for quite a while, but I knelt down next to him and felt his neck for a pulse. There was none. I listened to his chest for a heartbeat, but it was . . . so . . . very . . . quiet. Then I put my hand on his cheek and said, "I'm so glad you're in heaven now."

Every generation or so, an athlete comes along whose effect on people far surpasses his physical talents. Byron Nelson was one of those special people. His quiet faith in God ruled his life. What impressed and affected me most was that he led by example, not by preaching. We still all miss him here on earth, but you just know that he and the Lord are having some great times in heaven. If I should be so blessed as to walk through the Pearly Gates someday before my wife, Louise, the first people I want to see from my past are not my parents or other family members. I want to see Byron first. What a guide he will make!

Jay Morrish
Golf Course Architect and Friend

19

Aftermath and Media

The moments and hours after Byron's death went by in a blur. I couldn't reach Dr. Murphy or Jon Bradley, but fortunately Eddie was on his way back to the ranch from Denton, so he got there in about ten minutes. I was so grateful that Byron's golf cart shielded him from anyone's view, because when I called 911 and reported that Byron was dead, the scene became pretty chaotic, and of course the news media were all over it like human fire ants.

Yet there were so many sweet moments during this unhappy time: the first one was Eddie Baggs, Byron's strong right arm at the ranch, whose entire family Byron had baptized years before. For him to be so close to home when I called was a special gift. The next was one of our own Roanoke policemen on the scene when the ambulance arrived. When it was clear that Byron was really gone, and there were no signs of foul play, Sergeant Almonrode asked me which funeral home I wanted to call. The only one I could think of was Lucas in Fort Worth, because the last time we had been there to pay our respects to the family of a longtime friend, Wade Banowsky, Jim Lucas had welcomed us personally, and it was clear that Byron knew him well. As we left that evening, Byron said, "I like the Lucas family—they're good people."

So I told Officer Almonrode, "Lucas."

He immediately said, "I've got Jim Lucas's number in my cell phone. I'll call him right away."

As I made call after call the next hour or so, I was numb, simply trying to notify anyone and everyone who needed to know—Byron's brother, my family, the church. And I made it safely through the day. The Roanoke Police Department was absolutely splendid, setting up a roadblock to keep curious onlookers away, because the news was on the air within minutes.

One friend I made sure I phoned immediately was Tracey Stewart, because I didn't want her to find out about Byron the way she had found out about her husband, Payne, from television. When I called and told her, she instantly said, "I'll be there tomorrow."

I said, "Oh Tracey, you don't need to do that."

She replied, "Yes, I do; you're going to need help to get through this."

And I was truly grateful. She was such a rock, even helping me find things to laugh about through it all.

But there was no laughing that night. On the way to bed, I picked up one of Byron's work shirts, and his fragrance—his skin always smelled so wonderfully sweet—was in every thread. I began sobbing and went completely to pieces for a long time, it seemed, though it was probably no more than about a half hour. Then I could almost hear his voice saying, *Now, honey, you're going to make yourself sick. You've got to stop this.* So I laid his shirt on the other side of the bed and said, "That's going into the laundry tomorrow." And I slept the night through.

The next day my children came, and I will always remember my daughter-in-law Anne's sweet face, tears already running down her cheeks, as she came in the door with John and hugged me. Anne is a beautiful young woman of few words, but she makes every one mean something special. John and Stan were such stalwarts, keeping me busy and calm and helping field phone calls. The three of them even cleaned out and organized the garage. Stan's equally wonderful wife, Hope, had to stay in San Francisco and hold down the fort with their three children, but she sent her love as well.

Then Jenni New and Jamie Atchley came from our beloved Richland Hills Church of Christ, where we had been members since 2000. We both had always felt this was the congregation we had been seeking for a long time. Preacher Rick Atchley was amazing, so clear and strong and loving in his teaching of the Word, and there were so many ministries going on that Byron was in hog heaven, one might say, with so many choices for giving.

Byron had the unusual ability to know you're special and still stay humble and the desire to leverage personal greatness for others. He never stopped growing. He never settled. He finished strong.

Rick Atchley
Senior Pulpit Minister
Richland Hills Church of Christ, Fort Worth, Texas

The Farewell

Jenni and Jamie had come to help with the funeral planning, and since there was already a huge event scheduled at the building for Saturday, the service needed to be Friday, so we got to work quickly. Looking back I can now see that I was still in a state of shock, because when we sat down in the den to talk, I could only focus on the state of the rug on the floor, which badly needed to be swept.

I said, "Where is the vacuum cleaner?" out loud, and dear Tracey, sitting across the room, promptly got up and went to find one.

Then son John came in from the office to tell me Jon Bradley was at the door with a question about the funeral. So while I went to deal with that, Jenni shut the door between the two rooms, and the three ladies set about sweeping and doing who knows what else so I could get focused enough to help them.

This wasn't just a funeral for a church member; they had to plan for professional golfers, Salesmanship Club people, and folks coming from all around the country. They did a magnificent job, thanks to some great help from Jon Bradley, Janie Henderson, Bette Rathjen, and countless others.

Perhaps the greatest blessing of all came when John Willbanks, one of our elders, called and told me that Alistair Begg, the preacher at Parkside Church in Cleveland, Ohio, whom we listened to every day on the radio and who had even come to the tournament, to our home, and to our church the past spring, had said that if I wanted him to come and speak, he would. Of course I did.

The service was truly wonderful. Though I was still in a pretty strange state, I was able to put together a small talk to thank everyone and tell a little about life with Byron. I hadn't planned on it initially, but when I thought of dear Tracey and her courage as she lived through that nightmare of Payne's death, I thought I could at least do the same for Byron, whose passing was so much more peaceful and timely.

But to have Ken Venturi, Jon Bradley, Rick Atchley, Byron's nephew Ken Newell, and Alistair all tell wonderful stories of Byron and so clearly delight in his life was immensely healing for me.

One of my favorite memories of Byron is how he noticed a couple at our church. The wife could have had such a nice smile but had lost some teeth through the years. In his quiet, considerate way, because he didn't want her husband to feel bad about it, he asked me to find a dentist who could give her a beautiful new set of dentures, which cost Byron several thousand dollars. So I did, and honestly, it completely changed her life. She really did smile a lot more and was so much happier and more confident. When I saw her at Byron's funeral, she hugged my neck and said, "I had to come thank Byron one more time."

Mary Ann Izzarelli
Ebby Halliday Realtor and Friend

Moving Forward

Once everyone was gone and my life slowly, or quickly, depending on how you view such things, changed gears, I began to deal with all the things that Byron had done for me that were now my responsibility.

It wasn't all that difficult, because he had taught me enough about his business affairs and what needed to be done that I found the bill paying and so forth fairly straightforward. But once again I found that Mr. Nelson had a couple more surprises in store for me. He had died on Tuesday and the funeral was Friday, so I knew that on Saturday morning I needed to give Manuel, our ranch helper for fifteen years, his weekly check. I'd done it before and knew Byron never did it ahead of time, only on Saturday morning. So I got out the ranch checkbook, opened it to the correct page, and found Byron had already done it, apparently a day or two before he died. Then I saw that he had already made out a check to our church as well, plus several to church ministries. It wasn't spooky at all, just an extra blessing, as if he were saying to me, "See, Angeldoll, I'm still taking care of you!"

The following week was easier than I had expected, since I chose from the beginning to focus on how happy Byron was to be in heaven, seeing Louise and his family and Jesus face to face, and to just remember and be grateful for all the time we had together.

The Dream

However, the following Saturday, a week after the funeral, I was fighting sadness all day long, refusing to give in to it. But as I brushed my teeth that night, close to midnight, I began feeling like a five-year-old kid, and said out loud, "I know you want me to be brave, but I can't do it all the time!" I walked into our bedroom and sat on the edge of the bed, now crying as hard as I had the day he died. I pleaded, "Please let me dream about him; let me see him one more time!"

As my head hit the pillow, I remember noticing my clock said 12:01, and I was instantly asleep. Then I saw him, standing in a darkened hallway, with a warm golden light behind him.

I said, "Thank you for coming to see me; what is it like there?"

He replied, "It's music, and it's peace, and it's light."

And I woke up. The clock said 12:04. Now I'm not one to make much of dreams as a rule, because in my experience they have about as much to do with whatever I ate that evening as anything else. But wherever this one came from, it was such an instant answer to the most heartfelt prayer I had ever said in my life that I have thanked the Lord many times for the comfort and peace it gave me.

After that one difficult day and the gift of that dream, things became much easier, and I would find myself smiling and even laughing out loud at things Byron had said and done, including this: about four months earlier we were sitting in the kitchen discussing redoing the vinyl flooring and painting all the cabinetry. As we recalled the two weeks of utter chaos that had ensued the last time we had it done ten years before, Byron said, "Sweetheart, why don't you wait to do it till after I go to heaven?" So I laughingly agreed, and that's exactly what happened. But this time, I did the painting all myself, in a pale yellow, and talk about therapy!

I suppose the next most difficult thing to do was our annual Christmas letter, which I had been doing for fifteen years or so. This one was a little tough, but here's part of it:

Well, of course you know you're not going to live forever, but when you're married to someone who's always been so alive, it's virtually impossible to think about the not-forever becoming the now. We continued to delight in each other, spend as much time as we could together without being desperate about it, and we were so entirely, moment-to-moment happy! We knew we were blessed beyond measure to have had the time we were given, to have played golf together hundreds of times, traveled to as much of the world as we wanted, to have cuddled and kissed and held hands, laughed and smiled and ever so occasionally fussed . . . and then my sweetheart went to heaven . . . at the perfect time, having said the perfect thing to me just before I left for Bible class: "I'm so proud of you." . . . We were all so blessed to know and love this gentle champion, and my burden is easy and my yoke is light, because I'm being carried in the arms of the only One who has the answer to all of our questions.

Living in the Afterglow

Now that Byron's happily in heaven, I've been given many unexpected blessings from complete strangers who met or spoke with Byron for just a few moments and yet were so touched by him. When they shared these things with me, it always seemed like a gift beyond time. Here are two:

In February 2008, I was at the Ford dealership in Grapevine, having my car go through its 45,000-mile checkup. It turned out that, since I was almost 4,000 miles late, the whole thing took nearly twice as long as it should have, and though I was tempted to be a little frustrated with the situation, I chose not to, and was therefore twice blessed. First, the gentleman who offered to give me a shuttle ride home (which I decided against because it would just mean more time coming back to get my car when it was ready), told me he had lived in the Roanoke area for thirty-six years, and the first week he moved there he met Byron at the local convenience store. He was impressed with how down-to-earth and friendly Byron was, never acting like he was someone important at all. He saw Byron in town several more times and found him to be just as friendly and open and humble every time, and he was pleased to get to tell me that.

Then he left to help another customer, and I began visiting with Larry Ferrell, the service adviser. It turned out that Larry is a great golf fan and a four-handicap player himself, who took lessons when he was a youngster from Don January and heard many stories from Don, who admired Byron a lot.

Then, about eight years ago, Larry and his older brother got to come to the tournament, and while sitting on the grass around the eighteenth green, Larry felt someone's hand on his shoulder and turned around to see Byron standing there. Byron introduced himself (as if they wouldn't know who he was!), visited with the two brothers a bit, and asked them, "Are you having a good time?" Most touching of all, Larry said while he was not usually given to crying over people's passing from this life, even his own family members, that when he heard Byron had died, he did cry. And hearing that almost made me cry too. To realize how Byron's influence touched so many people from all walks of life is just an amazing blessing.

Then there was also this little happening: in January 2008, I was standing outside talking with my contractor and good friend, George Williams, when a small black pickup truck pulled into the driveway. A man got out, who looked to be in his late thirties, and said, "Are you Peggy?"

"Yes," I said.

"Well, I made a promise to God that someday I would find you and tell you what happened to me."

"Okay," I replied a little hesitantly, and George moved a protective step closer, neither one of us sure of what was coming next.

The young man said, "You're going to think this sounds crazy."

I replied, "Not yet." Then he told me this:

I used to drive a dump truck in this area, and I would pass by your house several times a week. Then one morning, over a year ago, I was coming along 114 and happened to look toward your house, and I saw this really bright light coming out of the sky and down right over your house. I'd never seen anything like it before, so I stopped, got out, and looked around to see what could be causing it, but I didn't see anything but clear sky all around except for that light. So I got back in the truck and kept going, and after a while I turned on the radio and heard them announce that Byron had died that morning.

Oh, my goodness.

As I've worked on this book, and especially as others have added their own memories and stories of life with Lord Byron, I've realized over and over how amazingly blessed I have been and how many lives he touched, most of whose stories I will never hear in this world. It has caused me to be in wonder at how often and how many ways God himself played a part in it all.

For instance, when I stood there in my living room in Dayton after realizing being a Methodist preacher wasn't in my future and asked out loud, "Okay, God, what do you want me to do?"

The spring after Louise passed away and Byron got the call to come back to Dayton to play golf, what was it that made him remember and write to me when we'd had no contact for five years?

How was it that I had taken just enough classes at the seminary, studied just enough Bible, been humbled just enough to be ready to become simply a Christian?

What part did the Lord play in those two tournaments at Charlotte and Philadelphia during Byron's streak that resulted in its being not just one, not just six, but eleven in a row and unmatchable by anyone, including Nicklaus, Palmer, and Woods?

How did that streak serve to elevate Byron in the eyes of the golfing world to such an extent that a tournament would be named for him and his Christian influence be extended so much further than it possibly could have otherwise?

There's a wonderful old movie from 1950 called *Stars in My Crown*, starring Joel McCrea, Ellen Drew, and Dean Stockwell, that shows the importance of example and perseverance in bringing others in our world to an understanding of how good and loving God is and how much he cares for each of us. I don't know if Byron and Louise ever got to see it, but it could easily be a parallel to the kind of influence

Byron had on many others, as you've seen from the stories included here.

For me all I can do is continue to emulate him as much as possible each day, because while I have trouble trying to reach the pinnacle of being like Christ in every way, being more like Byron seems a little more possible. Recently Marcia and I were visiting one evening, and as we talked about various things close to our hearts, Marcia suddenly said, "You're becoming more like Byron." Sweet friend. That's just about the highest praise anyone could ever give me. I was so very blessed, and so I'll close this small book with a variation of the prayer I now say several times every day, building on the one Byron taught me long ago:

Most gracious heavenly Father,
thank you for the love we shared
and the good times we always had together.
Thank you for every minute
I got to spend with Byron.
Amen.

Epilogue

Back in the Clubhouse

Imagine with me that we've just played eighteen holes and walked to the clubhouse together. We're sitting around with cold drinks, telling tall golf tales and listening to Byron's friends, family, and fans telling stories about Byron, reliving golf shots and other moments they had with him through the years. Here is a sampling of what you'd hear:

———————————

Byron taught me the importance of putting people at ease. I saw him hundreds of times walk into a room where he was the guest of honor—whether it was a small gathering or a large group—quickly find the person or two who seemed most lost or shy about saying hello, and make a beeline for them. He would introduce himself, ask them about themselves, tell a story and find some small thing they might have in common. He was so consistent about that . . . it was a beautiful thing to observe.

Angela Enright
Public Relations Director,
Four Seasons Resort & Club

Life with Lord Byron

Byron and I became friends in 1965 when Preston Trail Golf Club opened in North Dallas. I saw in him his unusual magnetic personality. He lived his faith with pride and comfort and had the ability to inspire people. He made friends quickly, and new acquaintances left feeling he was their new good friend. I've discussed this about Byron with many others, and we all agree we were fortunate to know him, and knowing him made us better people.

Charles Summerall
Investment Banker and Longtime Friend

I first met the legendary Byron Nelson when traveling with the late president of Abilene Christian University, Dr. Don H. Morris. We met with Byron at his beautiful ranch home in Roanoke, and I felt as if I had become his good friend at once. I learned, however, that he made everyone he met feel they were friends. That was Lord Byron's style! In 1984, it was my great privilege to be the coordinator of a special dinner in Dallas to honor Byron and Louise when so many of his friends became sponsors and hosts to endow the golf program at ACU. In the years following that evening, Byron faithfully sent various honoraria he received to ACU to continue to build that endowment fund, which now totals well over one million dollars.

Dr. Bob Hunter
Vice President Emeritus, Abilene Christian University
and Member, Texas House of Representatives

When I first got the job at ACU as golf coach, Byron called me on my cell phone and told me he was happy I was going to be the coach for *his* team. First, I thought it was amazing he called my cell phone and that it was a great compliment that Byron was pleased I was the coach of *his* team. When I played for ACU at the NCAA National Championship Tournament in 1990, Byron sent a telegram to us saying, "Good luck" to *his* team. I've always felt blessed to be part of Byron's team as a player and coach, and to me, the ACU Golf team will always be Byron Nelson's team.

Mike Campbell,
ACU Golf Coach, brother of Professional Golfer Chad Campbell

Since 1934, Byron would often stay in my grandfather's (William M. Harison) home during the Masters Tournament. In later years, Byron continued this tradition by staying with my father, Phil S. Harison.

The most unusual quality I saw in Byron was his ability to recall in minute detail practically every single golf shot of his professional career. These golf stories were fascinating, as he would describe his club selection, ball flight, and final chip in or putt on a given hole.

From Byron I learned patience and kindness. I always noticed how kind and patient he was to every individual person he met. As a past Masters champion, he would often visit the first tee to greet players and patrons. He enjoyed analyzing the players' swings and genuinely enjoyed spending time with others.

Phil Harison Jr.
Member, Augusta National Golf Club and Friend

Byron had the ability to prioritize and make a permanent and absolute commitment regarding the things that were important to him. He displayed this characteristic in every encounter I had with him. There was never any doubt as to Byron's commitment to his faith, to Peggy, and to helping others through his golfing accomplishments.

Byron was not private about his commitment. Everyone he encountered soon realized his priorities and what he stood for. The most remarkable part of it for me was how easy it seemed for him to be so absolutely unwavering. He simply did not ever deviate from his values and priorities, and it was very clear to us all that this would always be the case.

Walt Henderson
Salesmanship Club Member and Friend

I'll always remember a day when I'd made a bad decision in my job— had lost some money and was very stressed. I needed a friend, someone to listen and someone to pray with me. I decided to stop and ask Byron for advice. I knocked at the back door and he was there at his desk. Peggy invited me in and I told my tale of woe. Byron said, "Let's pray about this." He took the initiative to help me go to God for help. I'll never forget the kindness both he and Peggy showed me that day. Byron didn't give me just some religious talk, just looked me in the eye and told me to believe that God would help me. Good advice.

Tim Johnson
Fairway Ranch Neighbor and Friend

We met Byron and Louise at Jasper Park Lodge in Alberta, Canada, during the 28th Oilmen's Golf Outing. Byron was the guest golf pro that year, and Joann got to drive both of them around to see the sights for several hours that day. We formed a fast friendship and kept in touch over the next few years with cards and letters. After Louise's death in October 1985, we had to talk hard to get Byron to return to the event the next August. On the way to Jasper we stopped to see a waterfall, and a woman came up and spoke to Byron. I apologized, but Byron said, "If someone recognizes me, I'll take the time to visit with them—it's an honor, really."

Rogers and Joann Lehew
Friends since 1978

Byron Nelson and his life made an indelible impression on my life for at least seven reasons:

1. He was a man's man. 2. He had a deep and abiding faith in God. 3. He lived each day fully and completely. 4. He had a great sense of humor. 5. He was always a giver, not a taker. 6. He respected others. 7. Above all, he knew how to be a friend.

Byron helped design and develop Preston Trail Golf Club, of which I was an early member. He loaned his name to the golf tournament sponsored by the Salesmanship Club, the Byron Nelson Golf Classic, and I was a member of the club, so I got to see how much of his time and talent Byron gave to the club yet took nothing in return. All of us were better because of Byron.

Mike Massad Sr.
Salesmanship Club Member
Byron Nelson Golf Classic Tournament Chairman, 1978

The most striking thing we saw in Byron was his ever-present sincerity and kindness. He taught us through his daily walk with God what a true Christian should look like. And anyone who only knew Byron as a golfer really didn't know him at all. We truly miss him.

Mac and Kay McCaslin
Fellow Christians at Richland Hills Church of Christ
Owners of K & B Clock Shop, North Richland Hills, Texas

Uncle Byron always had such a steady personality and was so completely aware of everything and everyone around him. I admired how he could handle every situation the best possible way for all concerned.

The most memorable thing he taught me was that what made him so admired by all people was his character, his devotion to Christian values, not just giving lip service.

Being kin to Uncle Byron brought me a lot of special feelings, because of having somewhat the same name. I was named not only after him but also after his and my father's father, the original John Byron Nelson. I would get asked almost daily if I was related to him, and I got the feeling you get about your children when you're proud of them, because honestly, I never heard anyone say a single negative thing about my Uncle Byron. And these days, that's very special.

John Byron Nelson III
Nephew, Son of Charles and Betty Nelson

In 1981, I got the head job at Philadelphia CC where I'd been assistant years before, and in 1990, the club added nine holes and celebrated its centennial by inviting Byron to come, which he graciously did, along with Peggy. During this trip Byron was asked to go to the same hole where he holed a 1-iron shot during the second 18-hole playoff for the U.S. Open in 1939, so they could take some pictures. He picked up a 2-iron from a set of his new irons we had in the shop, and I grabbed a ball at the last minute. Byron went to the spot in the fairway where he remembered hitting that historic 1-iron, some pictures were made, then I suggested he move a little closer so the green was more visible for the photos. He moved about fifteen yards closer, standing now on a downhill lie, made some more pictures, then looked at me, winked and said, "I can't resist!" And without a practice swing or warm-up, he hit the ball. It was a perfect shot, flying right at the pin. Amazingly, it did almost go in, missing the flagstick by just inches and rolling a few feet past.

Tim DeBaufre
Golf Professional and Friend

Byron was so humble and always thinking about others, reaching out to encourage and support both younger and veteran pros. Many retired pros don't want to extend advice or help, but Byron was just the opposite. He helped me so much, giving me the confidence to be a better player. Byron was one of the greatest golfers who ever lived, but he was a finer man. Not only do I believe this statement, but I've also heard it said by other people many, many times.

I have so many memories of Byron, but the one I enjoy the most happened at the tenth anniversary of my charity tournament fundraiser at Quincy Country Club in Quincy, Illinois. Byron and I played Payne Stewart and Bruce Lietzke in a nine-hole match. I'm pretty sure it was Byron's last exhibition of any kind in front of a gallery. I remember the sixteenth hole, where Byron had a six-foot sidehill putt for birdie to tie Payne. We were all miked, and Payne really gave Byron a hard time, asking him if he was nervous trying to tie him. Byron's competitive side showed up right then, and he asked Payne to pay attention and watch this closely. He sized up his putt from both sides and proceeded to run it boldly into the back of the hole, pumping his fist as if he had just won the Masters again. Later in the day Payne, Bruce, and I broke down into tears, trying to express what a special thing it was to compete along with Byron—a very special day for all of us.

D. A. Weibring
Professional Golfer, Friend, and Partner in Golf Course Design

(Peggy: They had an auction before we went out to play that day, and Byron had brought along one of his recently reprinted *Winning Golf* books. The bidding went a little crazy and finally got to $600 with two guys vying for the prize. Then Byron offered to supply another one, personally signed and autographed, if the two top bidders would each give the $600. They did, so D. A.'s charity netted a total of $1,200 for those two books, and everybody came out a winner!)

I had the distinct pleasure of making at Byron's request a set of irons and woods with Byron's name deeply stamped on them, as was the tradition during his great era in golf. Byron told me how he first began to understand the principles of designing clubs, and it was after he'd played in the U.S. Open at Oakmont. He wasn't happy with his performance and was blaming it on his clubs. He wanted to buy another driver that he thought would surely resolve the problem. Louise told him, "Byron, I haven't bought a new dress or shoes or anything for over a year, and you've bought four new drivers. One of two things is true: either you don't know what kind of a driver you want, or you don't know how to drive."

Byron reflected on that for a short time and promptly went to work there at the pro shop on one of his older drivers, the one whose looks he liked the best. He began using a file to reface it and began to understand the basic physics of bulge and roll on face geometry. When he got finished, he used that same design for the rest of his career, and that was the design we copied on the Byron Nelson Series.

Roger Cleveland
Golf Club Designer and Friend

Uncle Byron was such a humble man, and through the years he allowed himself to be refined by many challenges. He weathered the storms of life, such as Aunt Louise's stroke, with grace, dignity, and a heart seeking to honor our Father.

One of the gifts I treasure about Uncle Byron is the way he took time to smell the roses. He was so excited to receive the smallest of gifts—a new wrench, screwdriver, whatever it might be. He always made a big deal out of these small treasures.

He taught me that he could dearly love Louise for more than

fifty years and then fall in love with yet another amazing lady and be devoted to her until the day he died. He was a man with a great heart, willing to be pliable in the Master's hand.

Sandy Mitchell
Niece

What more is there to say about this wonderful man . . . or any man? He was "willing to be pliable in the Master's hand," and the Master fashioned a beautiful servant-minded champion, who strove with all his heart to reflect the Master's untarnished image into the world. A man of faith. A man of kindness and honor and peace. The greatest gentleman to ever grace the gentleman's game . . . and my life. Byron Nelson, my hero, my dearest love.

About the Author

Peggy Nelson lived most of her first forty-two years in Ohio, then moved to Texas in 1986 to marry world-renowned professional golfer Byron Nelson. A writer by profession, Peggy worked for twelve years in advertising circles in Dayton, Ohio, and shortly after her marriage to Mr. Nelson, wrote a book chronicling the history of Scottish Rite Hospital for Children in Dallas. In 1992, she assisted her husband in writing his autobiography, *How I Played the Game,* and effectively retired from writing to enjoy life with her remarkable husband until his death in 2006.

Mrs. Nelson continues to live at Fairway Ranch in Roanoke, plays golf occasionally, does a little flower gardening, tends her small flock of chickens, plays the piano Byron bought for her for their fifteenth anniversary, and serves as a greeter at the Richland Hills Church of Christ where she and Byron attended since 2000. She delights in her many friends, in visits to and from her sons and their families, and in the thousands of happy memories she has of her beloved Byron.

*The story of professional
golf's greatest single-year
achievement recounted
tournament by tournament
by the incomparable
Lord Byron—winner of
11 in a row, 18 for the
season, with a 68.33
scoring average.*

BYRON NELSON
REMEMBERS 1945:
Golf's Unforgettable Year
WITH PEGGY NELSON AND RUSS PATE

Byron Nelson Remembers 1945

It was the most unforgettable year in all of golf's history. Byron Nelson won eleven straight PGA tournaments. In fact he won eighteen official tournaments that year with an astonishing scoring average of 68.33.

You can hear Lord Byron himself recount the story of PGA Tour golf's greatest achievement, tournament by tournament, on the compact disc in the back of this book entitled "Byron Nelson Remembers 1945" as he is interviewed by well-known golf writer Russ Pate. You'll delight in his warm, deep voice as he tells funny incidents that happened on the tour, recalls from memory the shot-by-shot progress of each of his consecutive eleven wins, and reveals insights into himself with vulnerable stories in his humble, Christian way.

Here are the eleven events you'll relive with this Texas gentleman rancher and one of the greatest golfers ever.

March 11	**Miami International Fourball**
	Won four 36-hole matches with Harold "Jug" McSpaden
March 21	**Charlotte Open**
	Tied Sam Snead at 272, 16-under, won a double 18-hole playoff
March 25	**Greater Greensboro Open**
	271, at 13 under, won by 8
April 1	**Durham Open**
	276, at 4 under, won by 5
April 8	**Atlanta Open**
	263, at 13 under, won by 9

June 10	**Montreal Open**
	268, at 20 under, won by 10
June 17	**Philadelphia Inquirer Invitational**
	269, at 11 under, won by 2
July 1	**Chicago Victory National Open**
	275, at 13 under, won by 7
July 15	**PGA Championship Moraine CC, Dayton**
	Defeated Sam Byrd 4 and 3, at 37 under for 204 holes
July 30	**Tam O'Shanter All American**
	269, at 19 under, won by 11
August 4	**Canadian Open**
	280, even, won by 4

In 1945, Byron also won the Phoenix Open, Corpus Christi Open, New Orleans Open, Knoxville Invitational, Esmeralda Open, Seattle Open, and Glen Garden Invitational. He was in the Top Ten thirty times, including second place seven times, and third place once.